THE QUESTIONS
GIRLS
ASK

THE QUESTIONS
GIRLS ASK

(Meyn)

By MARJORIE VETTER
and LAURA VITRAY

Inspired by the original book
by HELEN WELSHIMER

E. P. DUTTON & CO., INC.

NEW YORK
1959

CONTENTS

FOREWORD

The young person's problems cannot wait. Time is *now*. Lucky you, if you have learned to get happiness from the present minute. Few adults look back on their adolescent years as the bright, wonderful period of awakening and growth they should be. "I wouldn't live over again that time of confusion and misery for all the gold in Fort Knox!" is the common cry.

Unfortunately, for many complex reasons, these years are all too often bewildered, unhappy ones. But they need not be if you find the answers that will help you understand yourself and those around you and take advantage of your opportunities.

The Children's Charter, adopted by the United States in 1930, states nineteen aims for all the children of America —among them the right to be born healthy, to have a chance to develop a personality, to have the love and security of a good home, spiritual and moral training, education, protection against stunting labor, and to be members of voluntary organizations that supplement home and school experience. The charter lists these aims, but does not of course *guarantee* that each and every young person shall find himself in happy possession of all these fine things.

In order to find out what the current needs, interests and problems of adolescent girls throughout the country are, the Girl Scouts of the U.S.A. recently commissioned the research department of Michigan State University to make a national survey of girls eleven to eighteen. The

7

Girl Scout magazine, *The American Girl,* has a department, "What's on Your Mind?" to which readers send their problems. Last year over seven thousand letters asking for information and help were received from girls throughout the United States.

Based on the Michigan Study and on the most recurrent and universal problems in the letters from girls received by the magazine, the present editors have written this new book giving present-day answers to questions of current importance to teen-age girls.

If we have helped our readers to a better understanding of themselves and others, to adjust more easily to a society of men and women, to make the most of their talents and abilities, and to find these important years of growth and development a happier, more satisfying time and a better preparation for a rich, full adult life, we shall be grateful.

MARJORIE VETTER
LAURA VITRAY

THE QUESTIONS
GIRLS
ASK

CHAPTER ONE

THE RIDDLE OF YOU

*Can I improve my personality—change the things
in me I don't like?*

*Why am I suddenly so much taller than all my
friends?*

*Why do girls menstruate? Is it safe to bathe at
this time? How does a woman have a baby?*

*Is it wrong for me to want to be independent? To
disagree with my parents?*

*Why do I sometimes feel cross and blue for no ap-
parent reason?*

Questions, questions, questions! The girl you faced in the
mirror this morning was so full of them you felt dismayed.
You've been living with her for a number of years—
thirteen, fourteen, maybe even sixteen or seventeen—but
until now she never was so troublesome.

Now she says, "I want to know about myself. I must
begin thinking about my future. How can I be more
beautiful? More popular? How can I free myself from
dependence on my parents and start being *me?* What sort
of person am I—and what do I really want to do? Shall I
plan for a career? Will I fall in love and get married? Will
my life be as wonderful as I dream?"

The questions girls ask have answers, for any girl who

11

seeks them sincerely. And life can be as full and rewarding as you make it.

No wonder you ask questions in your teen years for you are on the threshold of great adventure. Childhood is over; adulthood, with all its enormous potentialities for achievement and happiness and self-realization, is just ahead. There's not a moment to waste if you are going to make the most of it.

Understanding yourself is a large order. It takes in your mind, your body, your emotions. And these aspects of the total YOU don't stand still while you study them. They are constantly changing. They have been changing ever since you were born—and the biggest changes of all come during the adolescent years. As a personality you will go on growing as long as you live. But the big push is right now.

Mentally, though you may not suspect it, you are really very, very old. You see, that fine equipment you have for clear thinking was handed down to you, not only from your parents, but from remote ancestors whose names you have never even heard. From them you inherited a brain, certain natural tendencies, an intelligence that educators like to measure and call your I.Q. They used to think an I.Q. was a fixed quantity, but now many are coming to believe that even that changes and improves, under the impetus of a determined effort—by you. So you need to understand that your mental *self* is like a clock that only works if you wind it—and that the key is *incentive*. Eager desire to accomplish any task that requires thought is half the battle won.

From the moment you were born, you found yourself in an environment that started pushing and prodding and seeking to mold your mental self and your emotions into a personality. At first it was only the influence of your mother and father that shaped your attitudes and your sense of values. Gradually the field broadened to include your brothers and sisters, the people of the neighborhood, your personal friends, your teachers at school. They have all registered their effect on you, often quite without your knowing it. To a certain extent, you are what they made of you. If it was a good environment, the result ought to be pretty good. And even if it was not all you could wish, the last word has not been written.

Now you are at a new stage: it is *you yourself* who are taking over. Not that you must throw overboard all the wealth that you have acquired, in thinking equipment, in mental and emotional controls, in attitudes and personality, since you began. The simple fact is, you could not if you would. But you can direct and modify it, strengthen it where it needs strengthening—build yourself an adult personality that is seaworthy for your voyage through life. That is your job in adolescence. Your urge toward independence is perfectly normal.

A young woman we know—we'll call her Helen—has just finished college with a brilliant record, and plans to become a schoolteacher. When we asked her what her father did, she replied, without embarrassment, "Dad is a farm laborer. He had only two or three years of schooling, and never believed it was worth while. When I got through eighth grade, he insisted I go to work. I won mother over to the idea of my entering high school, and she helped me gain Dad's consent. It was harder still when I finished high school and talked about college. Neither of them approved of that—but I managed to make them see that it was my life, and I was the one to decide. Now they're glad I did. They understand better—and they even boast about me! They're such grand people, but they'd grown up in a very backward area and they were always so very poor! How could they be expected to understand that the scholarship

I was offered and the odd jobs that have seen me through would open up a whole new world of opportunities? They believe it now."

It is easy to see that very early Helen formulated a vision of the woman she wished to become, and that her goal included a fine character as well as a fine education. That is why she was able to accept and profit by the good within her home environment, while asserting her independence.

You probably do not have such difficult problems as Helen's to face in your effort to achieve maturity and independence. But you do face obstacles. Quite naturally, you find that you are beginning to disagree with your parents on many issues that you regard as important. Until lately, you thought the bunch who are your close personal friends had all the answers, and you were inclined to go along with them in everything they decreed. But now you're beginning to disagree with them, too.

Some of these disagreements at home and elsewhere are worth examining—and we'll have a look at them later on. Right now, the important thing is to see how surely they indicate that your personality is growing—becoming adult.

Think back a little and you'll see how very far you've come. At three, you snatched the other child's toys and did not give one iota whether he or she liked you or not. You looked for affection and approval from Mother and Dad. When they frowned and scolded and seemed to withdraw from you, you were unhappy. And so they impressed their discipline upon you—made you stop snatching toys and smearing food on your face and walloping your little sister or a playmate, and behave nicely, as they themselves did. Slowly, even painfully, a new idea soaked down into your consciousness: that you were not the only person alive. It was not an idea that came into the world with you—and it was one you resisted for a long time. Because there were others with equal claims, you could not always expect the biggest piece of cake, the most rides on the tricycle.

Discipline, wisely imposed by your parents, created something new in you—a set of inner controls that today are as much a part of you as your hands and feet. You could compare them to the ruler that measures inches, or the scales that weigh things, or the kitchen utensil that marks off pints and quarts. These built-in controls of yours —some people call them a conscience—constantly measure how much you owe yourself and how much is due the other fellow. They measure selfishness and generosity, kindness and cruelty, love and hate, cheating as opposed to fair play. Because they measure things like that, they help you to solve all sorts of problems.

But now, let's see. People manage to get good results with different systems of measurements. The French measure dress goods with a meter rod that is approximately thirty-nine inches long. We use a yardstick that is only thirty-six inches. The standard is different, but the resulting dress can be just as pleasing and just as right, though each feels free to measure his own way.

It's somewhat the same with those built-in standards. When you were small you accepted your parents' unquestioningly; you knew just how Mother and Dad would measure your acts, even if they did not happen to be around. And that knowledge kept you out of a peck of trouble!

Later, as your social contacts broadened, you began to measure things a little differently, sometimes letting the standards of your group of close friends replace those imposed on you by your parents. You felt that parental standards might be a bit old-fashioned—just as the French might tell you that our yardstick is old-fashioned. You wanted to run with the gang, do what they approved.

This period represented progress toward maturity. It showed that you had generously indentified your happiness with that of others. It marked a little harmless experimentation in building standards of your own, and inner controls that did not have to lean on grownups.

Still, as an adult, you'll need something better to rely on. You won't always have your parents, or the gang, at your elbow to give you the word. You'll have to measure your acts and make your decisions for yourself. On the foundation you already have, you must now start building an adult personality, with its own independent, adult measuring system.

Someone has said that living creatures differ from stones by their ability to learn and to solve problems. You may have read of the monkey that solved the problem of reaching for food, placed too far outside his cage, by fitting two grooved sticks together. That was certainly clever for a monkey, wasn't it? But you are smarter than a monkey, and will have many more difficult problems than he to solve. You'll need more than a couple of grooved sticks. You'll need more than your parents' say-so, fitted neatly into that of the gang. Together, they might not reach far enough to solve all the problems you will meet as an adult.

One reason why adolescence is so challenging is that so many brand-new problems are bunched here. It's a period of accelerated growth—growth of your body as well as your personality. While your intelligence, your inner controls, your view of the world have been taking on new breadth and scope, your legs have been growing longer as well. You've been shooting up like a sunflower in the garden—or sometimes a bit unevenly, let's say like a bashful tomato plant.

For every girl, adolescence is the time of major physical changes. They are very important ones, designed to prepare you for full and useful womanhood. The body is having its special tune-up, so that glands and organs can function in ways that will carry out their purposes. Nothing new has been added: the delicate parts that were required to make you a whole and complete woman were there at the moment of birth. The time has come when they must be readied for their role of bringing new life into the world.

Recently, when researchers from the University of Michigan talked with girls all over the United States, in the survey they conducted for the Girl Scouts, they reported that most girls, no matter what other ambitions they might have, hoped to marry some day and have children of their own. You are probably no exception. Though women are entering many fields of work today, in full partnership with men, the role of motherhood has lost none of its importance. On the contrary, the latest findings of science show how vital it really is. Motherhood is a big job, and you in turn must bring to it your utmost in mental and physical fitness.

To do that, you need to know how your body functions, just as you need to understand your mental equipment. So let's have a look at the changes that occur during the adolescent period.

In either a boy or a girl, sexual maturity does not arrive suddenly, but rather slowly and after a period of preparation which is apt to begin with a spurt in growth. As this does not always occur at the same age, it may cause embarrassment to the girl who for a time towers above her classmates. Moreover, this growth stage usually occurs in girls earlier than in boys—thus creating one of the very special problems of adolescence.

Take the case of Claire, who had always been a bright and happy little girl, until in a fairly brief period she saw herself a "giant among the pygmies." Her best friends teased her about it, and she came to feel that she was no longer one of the bunch. She stopped going around with them, sat at home just watching TV or daydreaming, became absent-minded and inattentive in school, and sometimes quite impertinent when her mother and dad scolded her for bringing home poor reports.

But after a while, something good happened. Several of her former girl friends—and one boy in class as well—joined her in the bean-pole stage. As the others caught up, she felt better about herself, decided she wasn't a freak after all, and regained her happy, sociable disposition.

If that sort of growth spurt has happened to you, you know how it gave you an emotional jolt and a problem that had to be met. Of course, if you were prepared for it, you did not take it too seriously. Often these changes do happen in a fashion that seems erratic. A girl may for a time appear to be a "fatty" rather than a bean pole—as her chest enlarges from front to back, and the bony structure of the pelvis, that houses the uterus, broadens and deepens. But eventually everything works together to give the girl's adolescent body its womanly and adult contours. Similarly, the boys who yesterday were small and underdeveloped, will shoot up, become hard of muscle, broad-shouldered and narrow-hipped, with deeper voices and all that comprises the masculine allure.

One of the early changes in a girl is the enlargement of the breasts. Here, too, there is no timetable that is reliable. One girl may still be flat as the living-room wall while her best friend has developed a set of attractive curves. It can be exasperating—but fortunately, it is neither final nor fatal. Still, the emotional problem is hard for some girls to face. Some settle for a little padded bra that is harmless camouflage during the interim period.

Somewhere between the ages of thirteen and fifteen—though occasionally as early as ten or as late as sixteen—a girl reaches what is known as the menarche. This is the beginning of menstruation or the menses (meaning "monthly," from the Latin word for month.) Monthly is really an inaccurate term. When fully established, this routine of the female body normally occurs about every twenty-eight days except during pregnancy.

The female organs of reproduction, located in the abdomen, consist of the uterus or womb, where the future baby will develop; and the ovaries, two glands that appear like flat oval discs on either side of the uterus, and are connected with it by the Fallopian tubes. One of these discs produces an ovum (Latin word for egg) in each alternate month.

Only if the egg is fertilized by its counterpart, the male spermatozoön, can it develop into a human being. At the moment we call conception, these two microscopic cells unite to form a single cell, which, as the seed of the new life, has locked within it factors of inheritance from both parents.

Such a fertilized cell enters the uterus, where it lodges and begins at once to divide and multiply. The new cells thus created arrange themselves, first of all, in a long column that will become the spinal cord of the new baby, and one end of this column bends over to become the brain. From there on, in an awe-inspiring process of growth and differentiation of function of the dividing cells that no one yet has been able to explain, the whole tiny infant body begins to take shape. When one great scientist was asked whether he believed in miracles, he replied, "How can I help it, in the face of the miracle of birth?"

When, after nine months, the new baby is sufficiently matured to begin an independent existence, it is expelled from the uterus through the vagina or birth canal, the walls of which lie in deep folds that are readily expansible.

The ovaries produce a hormone which controls and regulates the menstrual flow of blood. Its purpose is to renew the lining or wall of the uterus and maintain it in condition to receive the fertilized ovum.

The beginning of menstruation does not necessarily indicate that a girl's body is fully ready for the function of motherhood. Moreover, if the flow is scanty, or irregular, as it often is at first, there is no great cause for concern. The tune-up of the whole organism, with its infinite complexity and the delicate balance between body growth and the specialized action of the organs of reproduction, takes time. When this process is complete, the girl has reached what is known as puberty.

Menstruation is generally heavier for the first two days, lasts about four days. You may have some small aches and pains at the beginning, but a healthy girl should be able to carry on at this time much as at any other, except for prolonged or violent exertion. If you continue to suffer undue distress, you should see your doctor.

Many of you ask about bathing, swimming, exercise at this time. Certainly you should continue your warm daily bath during this period when you especially need to keep clean and fresh. Cold showers or swimming in cold water had best be postponed. You need not forego short walks to school or other light exercise, but your own good sense would tell you horseback riding, long and strenuous hikes or violent competitive sports should be avoided. Tell your coach when you expect your period if you go out for sports, so that she won't ask you to compete when you should not overexert yourself.

Dorothy Clark brought on serious trouble later in life because she foolishly took long rides over rough mountain trails one summer, rather than tell her boy companions that she was not up to such strenuous exercise on certain

days. Although Dorothy would not discuss intimate physical details with her boy acquaintances, she should have felt
no embarrassment or hesitation in saying simply that she
was not feeling equal to a long ride that day—*period.*

Some of you may feel out of sorts, cross and blue at
these times. When you understand that it may be your
busy reproductive organs causing these mental attitudes,
you will be better able to conquer gloom and take such
feelings in your stride. This is the way to treat the whole
business of menstruation, for it will be with you for many
years. Don't allow yourself to be upset by momentary
discomforts. Accept them calmly as part of your life with
as little grumbling and inconvenience as possible. They
are small in comparison with the wonderful experience that
awaits you when someday you become a mother.

You may be right if you think that a girl's biggest problems during adolescence are mental and emotional. While
you are changing in appearance, you are likewise growing
and broadening in your social contacts. You have moved
out of childhood—given up paper dolls for parties and
perhaps having dates with boys. You are taking a new
look at a wider world—hoping for respect and consideration
and attention now that you are a young woman. You long
to prove yourself, gain status as an adult with those you
know, both at home and in school.

How to accomplish all this? At times you are deeply
troubled by your sense of inexperience. In daydreams you
see yourself as you would like to be: beautiful, poised,
surrounded by admirers, a skillful hostess, a good conver-
sationalist. But at the school dance you may turn out to
be a wallflower; the handsome boy about whom you dream
never even notices you—or if he should ask you for a dance,
you step on his feet in your confusion and fail to find a
single word to say. At home, your biggest cause of resent-

ment and worry may be that the family still treats you like a baby. Your growing sense of independence rebels at your being told to do household chores, or asked for a full account of all that went on while you were out with your friends.

Take heart. You are building an adult personality—and that is even harder, perhaps, than building a skyscraper. Some people never really make it, but you will! You will put in strong girders of character that can hold against the storms, and shining windows of friendship for many different kinds of people. You will be a woman—generous, free, loving life.

CHAPTER TWO

TAKE A SECOND LOOK

Can I make myself more attractive?
Shall I go on a diet to take off weight?
What can I do for a bad complexion?
Can you look pretty with a squarish face—a long
nose—a pointed chin?
How can I dress in order to look taller? Shorter?
Thinner?
Is it all right to wear lipstick to school?
What can I do to improve my dull, straight hair?

"But I hate the girl I see in the mirror," Betty says petulantly. "She's got everything wrong with her—everything! Why couldn't I have been beautiful, like Doris, or Kathleen? They have something—I guess you call it glamour. And are they popular! Especially with the boys!"

"Why don't you start being glamorous like them?"

"Who, me? Ugh! I never could, I've got everything wrong."

No, there's only *one* thing wrong with Betty—she is not willing to pay the price of beauty and charm and loveliness. She hasn't yet learned that almost everything worth having in life has to be paid for in some sort of coin—and so she is cheating herself.

We are not referring to beauty parlors, although we did

chortle at the sign we once saw in a beauty-parlor window: "Young man, beware! The beautiful girl you see coming out of here may be your grandmother."

Grandma's good points may be shading off, and the poor ones she started with are probably still there. With Betty, it's different. There are no crow's feet around her eyes, which are deep blue and wonderful—at least after a good night's sleep. There are no sagging muscles under the chin, no falling out of the thick head of light-brown hair, no stiffness in the joints to hamper her in a queenly walk. Trouble is, her wealth in the beauty bank is so great she squanders it as Grandma never would. As Doris and Kathleen never would, for they are too smart. Smart about beauty, that is.

But now, here is Betty, scrounging in a heap at the corner of the couch, in front of the TV set, munching a second slice of that chocolate layer cake she had for dessert at dinner. As a matter of fact, she's been munching snacks pretty regularly ever since she awoke this morning. No one could say she hadn't a good appetite, even though she did not manage to down her meat and vegetables at table. That was because she had stopped in with the bunch for a hot dog and coke after school. And then there were the chocolate nut candy bar and a few cookies snitched from the pantry while she was helping Mother by setting the table. Anyhow, she told herself, you shouldn't overeat when you are fat—and dinner comes so early! She rushed through it to get to the TV for a program she hated to miss. Pretty soon she must go upstairs and start her homework, or Dad will begin to scold. Why did they have to give all that homework? It's hard on the eyes, and a girl can't get enough sleep if she has to sit up all hours stewing over fine print. Afterward it's so late there isn't time for a nice hot bath and a hair brushing.

Betty isn't playing it smart, that's all. There's an old saying that beauty is only skin deep, but really it's a lot deeper than that. As deep as your general health, and all the good health habits it so clearly reflects. If the girl Betty sees in the mirror is overplump, with tired eyes, dull and unbecoming hair-do, sallow and perhaps pimply skin, it isn't because she cannot help being ugly. Not that at all.

If you want to practice independence through good self-discipline, here is the very place to start. There is nowhere that results will be so certain, so satisfying, and so unlikely to produce any arguments with Mother and Dad. Work out your own special program for becoming glamorous—and stick to it the way you would stick to a raft in a stormy sea. It *may be* a stormy sea, as you navigate those waves of temptation that beset you on every hand. But you will learn to ride them.

Your program will include both art and artifice. The art will consist of employing every sensible method for increasing your physical attractiveness *via health*. That is a big deal in itself, and is sure to require a lot of thought and work and will power to accomplish the best results. When it is well under way, you may still yearn for certain improvements that cannot be gained this way. You're too tall or too short; your cheekbones are too wide, your chin too pointed or your nose too large; your chest too flat or your legs too heavy. That's where the artifice comes in. Did you ever hear of an optical illusion—making people see *only* what you want them to see? The smart girl learns how to make herself into an optical illusion in which only the good points show up.

The art of being beautiful. Let's begin there. If you were building yourself a beautiful house, it would have to have four sound walls. Building a beautiful body is the same. The four walls are Diet, Cleanliness, Sleep, and Exercise.

Diet does not mean going without eating in order to make yourself slim. Of course you might survive for a limited time if you ruled out the basic foods, and merely consoled yourself with occasional snacks of hot dogs and cokes, cake and candy bars and ice cream sodas. But stop and picture how you would look. A beautiful body needs proper support for its tissues—so build the diet wall firm and strong, starting with a breakfast that sends you off to school with an "Oh, what a wonderful morning!" look on your face. Don't risk running into the captain of the football team with a hungry, half-awake scowl.

Every single day your diet should include: a serving of lean meat, poultry or fish; an egg; a leafy green or yellow vegetable at lunch and at dinner; citrus fruits or tomatoes or raw cabbage; some whole grain or rye bread; a couple of pats of butter; and three or four glasses of milk. If overweight is your worry, drink skimmed milk, or mix yourself a glass of one of the powdered milks on the market that have most of the cream removed. If there's a hole in your stomach between meals, fill it with an apple, a cucumber, or a stick of celery.

The body beautiful needs to be kept immaculately clean and sweet—or all its radiant allure will be blurred. So give close attention to the building of that second wall. It is a job to be worked at daily—not just now and then. For various reasons, cleanliness and careful personal hygiene are even more important in the teen years than at any other period of your life. In adolescence, due to changes in the skin, more sweat is secreted, and careful bathing becomes essential. Alice was chagrined to the point of tears when two of her best girl friends told her she suffered from B.O. Don't let it happen to you. The way to avoid such humiliation is to work out a schedule that allows time for splashing in a good sudsy bath each day—preferably at night, with a quick, refreshing shower each morning.

In addition to the bath, a good deodorant should be part of your daily routine. Use it after that morning shower—and then slip into the nylon scanties you flipped through a bowl of suds last night.

The face you see in the mirror will never delight you— nor anybody else—if you wipe it morning and evening with a soiled washcloth. At night, massage it gently with a lather of pure soap that will carry away dirt and dead skin cells, using your own clean hands and a little warm water, followed by cold to close the pores. Then put on a bit of some good cream to provide it with lubrication.

And what about your hair? Yes, it needs careful cleansing, too. Once a week or oftener, depending on its oiliness. Shampoos today are specially made for dry or oily or normal hair—so watch what you buy. And don't omit brushing with a good, stiff hairbrush, nightly and especially before each shampoo.

If you have to skip a TV show on school nights to make room for your cleanliness program just consider what you want most, mystery tales or glamour. It's just possible you can't have everything.

That's especially true if there is homework to be done as well, for your third beauty wall is waiting to be built. You've guessed what it is: a good night's sleep. Leave the burning of midnight oil to persons past sixty whose faces, perhaps, are becoming wizened anyhow. Your purpose is to greet the world with radiant complexion and shining eyes and a lilt to your laughter that weary people never display. The prescription for that is: eight to nine hours of good sound sleep, during which the crew of repair mechanics inside you rush around getting everything shipshape for the following day. Give the night shift a chance to do a thorough job, while you relax in soothing dreams.

Are we up to the fourth wall—exercise? A foreigner once referred to Americans as people who like to go on a hike sitting down! Could that be you? Of course you ride the bus to and from school—it's a whole mile. When you were ten everyone called you a tomboy—you were always doing something active like swimming or skating or playing hand-ball or climbing trees. As a teen-ager, you've become so feminine you scarcely stir except for dancing at a school party, and that doesn't happen every day. Athletics do not appeal to you any more—on "gym" days you often manage to be excused. "I'm tired. I don't have proper coördination. I guess I'm just awkward, and it's so embarrassing!"

No, you're not awkward. You may bump into a chair at a party because you're worried about your lack of social experience—but you have every whit as much motor control as you had at ten, even though you may be a bigger girl now. So banish that alibi. Remember this: there is no such thing as the body beautiful without exercise—in the gym and in the fresh air. Get up and out and give your lungs a chance to expand and absorb the ozone, your legs and arms a chance to stretch, your spine a chance to untwist. The feminine curves you aspire to need not be in your backbone.

No, a straight backbone and perfect posture are *musts* for the girl who would be regarded as beautiful. Take Mary. Everyone agrees that she is stunning. And yet, on close analysis the experts would surely never select her as "Miss America." What is it that makes the onlooker blind to her defects, and full of admiration? Why, simply her tall, straight, graceful figure, her erect carriage when she moves across a room, the tall yet easy way she sits in a chair. Of course, Mary did not come by all this without effort. She realized her features were a bit plain, her blue eyes a trifle heavy-lidded. But she watched the actresses in the movies and on TV, and saw that much of their glamour was in the way they handled themselves—walking, sitting, rising from a chair. Mary decided to attend a gym and work at these things every free moment she had. And she got results. She learned to imagine a plumb line running through her head and the middle of her chest, hips and feet, with "sky hooks" holding up her weight from the waist. She learned never to let her weight slump back on her hips and heels—but to walk with a free, clean-limbed stride from the hips, her legs just brushing, and moving back and forth as if they carried no weight on them. She kept her feet toeing ahead, pointed neither in nor out. Mary had fun "learning to walk"—and she could tell you that posture spells glamour in anybody's book.

So there is your health and beauty program, if you have the gumption to adopt it. Good diet, good hygiene, plenty of sleep, and exercise.

Add up your dividends and see how the investment pays. *Radiant complexion,* because the flesh underneath the skin is nourished by the right food, while the pores of the whole body are getting rid of waste by means of soap and water, and absorbing oxygen through your lungs. *Hair* with a glorious sheen; *eyes* that are clear and bewitching as the stars; a *figure* others envy because it is firm of muscle with no flabby fat; the straight, proud *posture* of a young pine tree that sways gracefully but is not bent.

It's a fine beginning. But here's poor Betty complaining that we have found no cure for some of her worst beauty defects. "My face is too wide, my nose is too big, my hair is too straight. I seem to be growing sidewise instead of up, and my legs are ugly. I can't change these things— and I'm just a mess!"

All right, Betty—and all the other Bettys with complaints of every kind. What you can't change you can camouflage. And so we come to the most fascinating topic of all: highlighting your good points, and hiding the bad ones so successfully that they sink into the background. Let's see how it works.

Beauty's artifice. Go back to the mirror and we'll start at the top, with faces and hair-dos. There are various designs for faces—some oval, some quite round, some very long with a high forehead, still others almost diamond-shaped, with a tiny little tapering chin.

It's an old conviction that oval is the only perfect one. But if you have one of the others, don't sigh, for it can be just as pretty, if properly framed. True, the oval gives you more choice of hair styles. With the other shapes, you need a bit more strategy.

A very round or squarish face might wear a pompadour of curls at the top of the bared forehead, with the hair brushed back smoothly at the temples, avoiding any impression of fluffiness. The long, narrow face requires the opposite—bangs on the forehead to cut its length, and fullness around the ears. A side part and side bang can be helpful in camouflaging a too large or too long nose, and if you wear a pony tail, be careful not to line it up with the tip of your too pointed nose. Keep it high at the back of your head, to improve your profile.

Your hair part can do a lot in camouflaging length or width, so try some experimenting. Of course a part right in the center will lengthen your face, and that may be what you need. If your face is too round, try starting at the crown of your head and tracing the line forward till it is over the center of an eyebrow.

If your face is diamond-shaped, with a small pointed or receding chin, fluffy curls at the nape of the neck will do a lot for you. Keep the hair full at the sides, but flat on top, probably with a center part.

Simple styles are best for the busy teen-age girl, and straight hair can be very becoming if glossy and in fine condition. But if you need waves, practice until you are an expert at pin curls. (Of course no girl who is interested enough in developing an attractive personality to read this book would ever appear in public—on a bus, subway or the street—with her hair in pin curlers.) There are home permanents available that are very easy to use. A good idea is to get some of your girl friends together for a home-permanent "party," in which you help one another to carry out the directions which come on the package. If possible, once a year make a trip to a beauty parlor to have your hair cut and styled. It's a good way to find out what an expert advises for your particular face.

Do you wear glasses? Don't despair! They are as beautiful as jewels today—and a positive improvement to many faces. Lucky you if your budget will stretch around a simple pair for school, in frames toned to the color of your eyes, and for party wear one of the sparkling lovelies that are as becoming as any of your accessories. In having them fitted, be sure they do not hide your eyebrows, an important accent to your face. And wear them with confidence, as you would a string of pearls, for they are in fashion. The girl who squints never will be.

If you've been eying yourself in a full-length mirror you are probably just panting by now to enter a whole new string of complaints. Too tall; too short; too fat; too thin! "I'm flat as my mother's ironing board and my friends have such grown-up curves. Is there anything I can do to develop my breasts?"

We'll take that question first. Nothing will make your breasts more curvaceous until the time comes for their development. But you can make them *appear* bigger by exercises that strengthen your muscles and improve your posture. Even walking and deep breathing will help. For straight camouflage, there's the padded bra, the dress with a big circular collar or dickie or large lapels, or a dozen other dressmaking touches you can invent for yourself.

And that brings us to the sewing machine—the most reliable aid to artifice in the beauty department a smart girl ever had. Ask your mother if you may do a little stitching on hers. She'll be proud as you are of the economical wardrobe you turn out, and the glamour you acquire through it.

Some of the greatest dress designers in the world have earned their reputations by making fat women appear like sylphs and bean poles like curvaceous sirens. The way they do it is through color and line that trick the eye. Take your cue from them.

We have just seen how faces can be "lengthened" or "broadened" in the illusion they give. The same principle applies to the whole figure. The girl who is plump is not led astray by a craze for puffed sleeves and a broad cummerbund, nor does she permit herself to be seduced by a big colorful plaid material that will give her the appearance of a brick house on wheels. She chooses materials that are monotone, or with stripes that can be worked up and down; and patterns that have a lengthening effect, perhaps by the diagonal line of a collar, or the slight hem-flair of a not-too-tight and never-too-full skirt. She's pretty sure to drop the hem line a trifle lower than that of her thinner friends—both to add length to her figure and to help camouflage her calves, that may be on the fat side. A slightly darker tone of stocking will also help there.

The overplump girl is aware of the wonders color can work. For her, perish the thought of gay contrasting blouse and skirt, even though she envies them on someone else. She elects lovely soft muted tones that remind you of the woods at twilight, or the blue sky at dusk. Her blouse or sweater is made or selected to blend with the tone of the skirt, with no fancy belt to give a crosswise line.

Plumpness may be due to unwise diet, lack of exercise, or merely to a passing stage of adolescent development. Only very rarely indeed has it any cause more serious than one of these. But while you have to live with it, be smart. Choose colors that dramatize the tones of your eyes and hair, and materials in monotones or stripes, or very, very tiny and inconspicuous designs. Plan your wardrobe in front of a mirror, before moving to the sewing machine.

Maybe you are the bean-pole type. You've sprouted fast, and now you are cultivating stooped shoulders to make you look shorter. Please, not that! It's the death of glamour! Picture yourself as a queenly actress sweeping into the spotlight, not as a loping kangaroo.

You cannot shrink—but you can make the bystander believe that you have. For you, bold color contrasts are quite the thing, and big sleeves, and wide belts. You love to don reds and yellows that dramatize your personality while they add to your appearance of weight rather than height. You know, too, that the clear pastels will do a lot for you. In dress materials, you can be easily tempted by the polka dots and plaids. The full circular skirt is especially for you who are tall. If you buy a suit, one in a lighter tone—beige or French blue or gray—will be most becoming.

Once you get the idea of what color and line can do to make you beautiful, you'll never give up the adventure of seeking the things that are right for you. Remember, you are the artist. Consult your mirror and decide what your good points are—golden, auburn or dark brown hair; olive skin, or one that is peaches-and-cream; pearly teeth and a pleasant smile? Make the most of these, while you conspire to underplay everything you dislike. It's what every great actress does. It's what every great dress designer strives for. With practice, you can become an expert at beauty's artifice.

What about physical defects? This brings us back again to health. Yours, we hope, is excellent—but there are occasionally physical defects and ailments that require attention and should not be overlooked. Medical studies have shown that 45 per cent of all young people between the ages of fifteen and nineteen have slightly diseased tonsils. Many others have infected teeth that are pouring poison into their blood stream, producing irritability and fatigue. Teeth that are crowding one another into a bucktooth pattern had better wear a brace for a short time in the early teens, for the sake of beauty later on. It's the price you have to pay for glamour! As for eyes—and ears—don't ruin your looks and your disposition by trying to hide anything that may be wrong with them. Hard-of-hearing aids today are inconspicuous as never before—they have taken on the camouflage of beautiful eyeglasses.

An occasional pimple is the rule, rather than the exception, during adolescence, often managing to sprout on the day of the big date. And that is true, even though pimples and blackheads usually yield to a wise regime of diet, cleanliness, sleep, and exercise. In such an event, you can camouflage the blemish for an evening with one of the inexpensive preparations on the market that do a neat and reliable cover-up job.

Serious acne, if persistent, needs a doctor's attention, in order that your skin may not be permanently scarred. There are also a few adolescent girls who are troubled and humiliated by a growth of hair on the face. Bleaching with a little peroxide may help, but such hair can only be permanently eliminated by electrolysis. Get your doctor's advice.

We're up to cosmetics. Touchy topic if ever there was one! Mary complains that her mother will not allow her to wear lip rouge at fourteen. Agnes wears it to school every day, and often can be seen dabbing it on between classes. What's the story?

Certainly a touch of lip rouge adds an accent to a pretty face, when neatly and discreetly applied. For parties and dates, a great many girls are using it by the age of thirteen. Choose it in one of the lighter or pinkish tones suited to your youth, and apply it carefully. The best way, for neatness, smooth effect, and an even line is to use a lipstick brush. Especially for dates, you may also wish to dab a speck of powder on a nose that is inclined to develop a shine. But heavy make-up and blotches of red applied to your cheeks in the teen years are as ridiculous—and unglamorous—as if you appeared in your grandmother's spectacles.

Some schools frown on the use of lipstick in classes— though some permit it. Here, a good rule is to abide by the general practice in the school you attend. If you and your classmates do wear it, make sure it is light and unobtrusive —and applied at home, or in the powder room, not in the classroom.

Lovely hands often profit by a nice manicure and a touch of pink nail polish that goes well with the lip rouge selected. Terry says she stopped biting her fingernails after she decided she needed them in her beauty campaign. She does not go in for long claws, in dark red as if they were dripping blood. Instead, she keeps her nails nicely rounded, well scrubbed with a nail brush, and the cuticle pushed back with the corner of the towel each time she gives her hands their careful washing. Her nails are the "happy ending" to a story of hands she keeps soft by the frequent use of a good cream or lotion. "I used to want to sit on my hands at parties," Terry confesses with a laugh. "Now I dare to let them show, and I feel less awkward."

Of course she does. Hiding your hands is harder than the attention it takes to make them beautiful.

By the way, in summer time, there are toenails, too, that emerge from open-toed shoes. They should be filed square —not rounded—and will take a little deeper tone of nail polish than your fingernails. We hope you have not developed misshapen toes or even corns by wearing too small shoes. When applying the polish, slip a little tissue between the toes, to prevent smearing.

And so—here comes the bandbox girl—YOU! You may be off on a healthful hike in dungarees. You may be trotting through the rain in a sun-and-rain coat chosen to give you colorful allure on a dull day. You may be off on a date in a lovely but inexpensive little creation you made yourself. But—there's one thing about you in every circumstance: you're appropriately dressed. You're dressed for your type. You are what you want to be and can be: glamorous.

CHAPTER THREE

YOU AND YOUR PARENTS

Must I tell my parents everything I do?
How old should I be to be allowed to have dates
  with boys?
How late should I be permitted to stay out on a
  date?
Should I be allowed to select my own clothes?
When I have my license, should I expect to use the
  family car whenever I wish?

"What's wrong with me?" Mary Kay asks. "Sometimes I have the most awful guilty feeling that I don't love my parents as I used to. We never see eye to eye any more, and we can't even talk things over without quarreling."

There is nothing wrong with Mary Kay. She is a healthy, normal fourteen-year-old. But she and her parents are living through a period of adjustment that can be pleasant or extremely trying, according to the understanding and restraint with which they handle it.

When Mary Kay was a small baby she depended on Mom and Dad for everything, tried her best to imitate them and felt secure and cherished in the warmth of their love. School widened her horizons and gave her a chance to have her first away-from-home experiences on her own, to begin to make her own choices. Now in her teens she feels the need to be independent, to stand on her own feet, be her own boss, make her own decisions. She rejects rubber-stamping anyone else's ideas and insists on her right to develop a personality of her own.

Mary Kay's mother and dad are trying to accept all this. But it isn't easy for them to face the fact that they no longer fill the important place they once held in Mary Kay's life. It is hard for parents to step aside, to give up the satisfactions of taking care of their children, and the feeling of being necessary.

Your parents, accustomed to protecting you, are fearful for you. They know, for all your grown-up appearance, you have had only the limited experience of youth. They want to save you from making mistakes; they are concerned about your future. Sometimes they add to the difficulties of the situation by thinking they can continue to direct your life, make your choices for you and determine the way ahead.

Mary Kay's mother and dad are also Jane and Jim—two people with personalities of their own. As you outgrew your fairy tales, you realized that in real life the marriage ceremony does not guarantee a life of untroubled bliss forever after. Now you are learning that motherhood and fatherhood do not magically change men and women.

Parents are sometimes tired, harassed, ill, troubled. They are not always sure of themselves and they do not always know all the right answers. You are one of their big worries. Have they done all they should for you? Have they made mistakes with you? As they see you striking out for yourself, they are afraid they are losing you. When you realize this, you will find it easier to give them the right you permit other human beings: to be themselves, to have faults, to make mistakes. As you come to appreciate their fine qualities, forgive their weaknesses, and love them for themselves, you will have taken a big step toward maturity.

Let's face it. You are not always a model daughter. Perhaps you are forgetful, untidy, and once in a while behave like a spoiled baby. It is not surprising if these things cause flare-ups.

You may envy Sally because her mother and father are so easygoing; Fran because her parents are so rich and indulgent they shower her with everything. Wise or foolish, strict or indulgent, your mother and father, as they really are, are a fact of your life that no wishful thinking will change. You have to get along with them, on good terms or bad. Why not choose the good? The teen years are an important period in a young person's relationship with parents. At this time the foundations of lifelong adult friendship, based on mutual confidence and respect, can be laid—or parents and children begin a drawing apart that widens into an impassable gulf.

Tears, temper tantrums, sulking will be evidence that you are still the baby you are trying so hard to prove you are not. Never try to settle a disagreement during a heated argument. Wait until calm is restored and then talk things over quietly. You may be amazed at how smoothly conflicts can be handled when you show you want to keep your parents' confidence, but make your own decision with their advice and help.

If you are mature enough to appreciate your parents' point of view and to realize that although you are almost grown-up you do lack experience, you will not try to win your independence by a continuous battle. Are you really behaving as grown-up as you want them to think you are? Surely a tornado must have hit your room to leave it in such a mess! Could it have been you who promised to be home at ten-thirty last night and then breezed in at a cool eleven forty-five? At the time you thought it maddening of

Dad to make such a fuss, and of Mom to remark that you lack consideration. But this morning when you have had a chance to think it over calmly you have to admit that perhaps your resentment was unjustified. You resolve to talk it over with your parents at lunch. You'll tell them that you know they were worried about you last night and you are sorry. You want them to have confidence in you, and you are going to try to earn it.

You will have to show them that you are capable of disciplining yourself if you want them to relax their controls. You must prove that you are ready to accept responsibility and to have regard for others. You must give up the idea that you should always have exactly what you want. Freedom, you will learn, does not mean license.

When the Girl Scouts conducted their interviews with girls all over the country in what is known as the "Michigan Study," they found that the younger adolescent girls were having arguments with their parents about make-up and clothes. Later, their troubles centered around dating, driving, smoking. At all ages, they seemed to run into trouble over allowances, curfew, and the use of the telephone.

Many of these questions are open to debate. They are matters of custom and locality.

Take the matter of lipstick. You would not want to be the only girl in your class to use it, any more than you would wish to be the only one not permitted to do so. Most parents allow their daughters to follow the local custom. They understand how hard it is for a girl to be different at an age when conformity is all-important. Possibly they permit it at first for dress-up occasions only. Your mother can be very helpful in selecting the right shade and showing you how to use it properly.

Disagreement over clothes? Give Mother's side some thought. She may be trying unconsciously to keep you a little girl too long. In that case, talk it over with her on a friendly woman-to-woman basis. Ask her to discuss it with her friends, and the mothers of your friends. Urge her, when she attends school affairs, to give careful consideration to the clothes your classmates wear, and cast her own private vote for the best-dressed girl. Show her fashion magazines—for your own age, remember, not your big sister's. It may surprise you how quickly Mom can become your ally in this clothes controversy.

There is also the other face of the coin. Midge Potter fell completely under the spell of Elaine Carter, a young married woman who moved into the neighborhood. Midge was thrilled, as the junior prom came up, to have a date with a good-looking boy in her social studies class. She wept and ranted and permitted her mother no peace until she gave in and bought Midge a copy of the daring black sheath Mrs. Carter had worn to a banquet. Midge did not have Mrs. Carter's figure, and the dress kept slipping off her shoulders. She was conscious of the raised eyebrows of the chaperones and her escort's embarrassment. The mistake, from which her mother had tried to save her, turned what should have been a never-to-be-forgotten evening into a nightmare.

Sometimes Mother really does know best and it pays to follow her advice. She knows you won't go wrong in the matter of dress if you stick to simple lines, go easy on jewelry and fussy accessories. Remember that understatement is often the most effective. You'll be safe on most occasions if you are under rather than overdressed. It's smart to look your age and leave the lace-curtain, "play lady" costumes to the kid stuff you've outgrown.

"Call me tonight." Could it be you—that teen-ager on the small of her back with her blue-jeaned legs up-ended over the arm of a chair, chatting for hours on the tele-

phone? Maybe your mother is waiting to phone her order for food, if she can't get to the supermarket. Or she'd like to invite some guests by telephone. It's possible she sometimes relaxes by chatting a few minutes with a friend over the telephone during the day. You, young imitator that you are, have grown accustomed to using the phone for discussions about clothes, boys, tomorrow's lessons, with friends you left only a short while earlier at school. And, of course, your boy friends call you to talk over the tennis tournament or next Saturday's date.

Some parents have declared certain hours—dinnertime, for instance—closed season for this sort of thing. If you have only one phone, there's no argument about the fact that it is a convenience to be shared by the whole family. Nothing is more likely to cause your dad to blow his top or turn an unsympathetic ear to your plea for a special favor than to have missed his train that evening because he kept getting a busy signal for thirty minutes while he was trying to call your mother. It's a wise daughter who does not abuse her telephone privileges. Talk over with your parents the hours at which it is best for you to make and receive calls. Then, stick to your agreement. You won't lose face with your friends if you call a halt in a reasonable time.

"Now that I'm a teen-ager, how much allowance should I expect?" A good question! You've been accustomed to running to Dad for everything, and now you feel that you are old enough to handle your own money—and you are right. You should be learning to do so.

Your allowance is a matter for family conference. The amount will be governed by the family's finances and what the money is expected to cover. If it includes church, school and social expenses, possibly clothes and personal needs, you will have to budget carefully and exercise your new self-discipline in living within it. Emergencies, when you are obliged to appeal to Dad for help, should not be allowed to happen often. If you are permitted to buy some or all of your own clothes, don't be above asking your mother's advice. Also how about earning money of your own by baby-sitting or other odd jobs?

Dating. We don't need to send out spies nor even to eavesdrop to know how important this is to you, or how often it is the cause of trouble with your parents. Of course you are eager for dates. Your teen years are the time when you should be getting to know boys (in the plural), and learning how to get on with them in a more grown-up relationship. To give you this opportunity many junior high schools have monthly or weekly dancing parties. The girl who is forced to postpone this experience until after high school sometimes finds it impossible to catch up with her classmates, and often is never able to enjoy male companionship on a comfortable basis in later life.

Some parents do not understand this, are reluctant to admit their little girls are growing up, or do not realize how early dating often begins today. If yours are uneasy about it, talk it over with them quietly, explaining where you want to go, and giving them the opportunity to meet the boys you want to date. Perhaps a favorite relative, teacher, Girl Scout leader, or clergyman could be persuaded to discuss the matter with them.

There is no set age for the first date, any more than for the first touch of lipstick. It all depends on the customs in your community and on how grown-up you are. Besides, a date can mean many different things. It may be walking home from a junior high dance with a boy classmate and stopping for ice cream, or having a coke with another boy and girl—or it may be the more serious dating of your college sister.

Parents can be helpful in introducing you to sons of their friends and planning your first boy-and-girl parties with you. It is up to you in your turn to keep to whatever rules they may make.

Karen's parents wanted her to have all the fun she could, but they expected her always to let them know where she was and to be at home by a certain hour. Karen appreciated the interest they took in her good times and their concern for her. She was careful to telephone and let them know if she changed her plans, and she made a point of being at home a little before the appointed hour. She built up such confidence in her responsibility and good sense that she had no trouble in winning the privilege of a later curfew hour for important occasions like proms as they came along. At such times she set the alarm clock for the hour she had promised to be home. When she came in she turned off the clock. In this way, she felt that her parents would not need to spend a sleepless night worrying about her, while she was having a gay time.

Most girls agree with their parents that dating on school nights is out, except for unusual occasions. Even seniors feel that midnight is late enough for ordinary week-end dates. Such glamorous affairs as proms, or college dances for the older girl, can be an exception. Boys, who have parents of their own to please, won't be surprised that your parents expect you to be home on time.

What about smoking? There really should be no conflict over smoking and driving. Most high schools have rules against smoking on the premises. Girls and boys who go out for sports are expected not to smoke. The temptation to sample a cigarette may be great—but you don't need any parental veto to tell you that at least until you are out of high school, smoking should be taboo for both health and social reasons.

If you are with a group of high school young people who believe they are proving their sophistication by smoking, here's your chance to assert your independence. No one will think less of you, and you will rate with the more mature boys and girls. The same thing is true with older girls in regard to drinking. Alcohol is a tricky and dangerous thing, and it makes sense to avoid it. The right kind of boy will respect your wishes.

Driving? Maybe your differences with your parents center around the family car. It is an expensive item. It belongs to your father and mother and they are liable for any damage caused by it. The age for obtaining a driver's license varies in different states. Many high schools have courses in driver education. Enroll in one if you can. When you have your junior license, read the restrictions on the back, and obey them without making it necessary for your parents to enforce them. Act as if you know the car belongs to Mother and Dad and they may be cooperative about letting you have it on special occasions.

Pat was ski champion of her high school. Her parents objected to her riding around with a boy who was a hotrodder. Pat was with him the day he hit a truck in passing another car at high speed on a curve. Her right leg, broken in several places, was so seriously damaged that she could never ski or dance again. She would walk with a limp for the rest of her life. If only for your own selfish sake, heed your parents' restrictions about your own driving and that of the boys you go out with.

Your parents and your parties. Maybe you complain because your parents will not let you have a party unless they are on hand. "This isn't the gaslight era!" you sputter. "I'm no baby, and I don't need a chaperon." All the same, you should ask your parents to be at home when you entertain, if for no other reason than to show that you know the proper etiquette. Explain tactfully that they need not endure an entire evening of rock and roll, but you want them to be inconspicuously on hand somewhere nearby.

To be friends on an adult basis with your mother and father pays off in satisfaction all your life. It isn't automatic. You all have to do your part. You have to learn to give as well as to take in all relationships. Throughout life you will be meeting different kinds of people with different characteristics. You won't always be able to have things your own way. You will find it easier to get along with your college classmates and teachers, your business associates, fellow club members, your boss, your husband and even your children, if you begin now to practice acting like a grownup. Some adults never attain what psychologists call emotional maturity, but you will if you make the effort now to get along with your parents. You'll be thankful all your life, and those near and dear to you will be too.

CHAPTER FOUR

SIBLINGS

How can I make my big brother stop teasing me?
What can I do about my untidy younger sister who
shares my room and borrows my clothes?
How do I stop my small brothers and sisters from
raising a racket when I have guests?
Should I expect to be paid for baby-sitting my
siblings?

Siblings—that means brothers and sisters. Sometimes it
means problems, too! But it's wrestling with problems that
makes you strong, teaches you to assume adult responsibilities, and speeds you on the road to true independence.

Sometimes, to be sure, a girl may feel that in the problem area, she has an extra supply. And she may tell you
that it's not her parents, but her brothers and sisters who
are the biggest problem of all. Here she is, struggling to
build a personality, a *self* she can respect, and they seem
bent on preventing her from doing it. If she appears at
the dinner table with a new and more becoming hair-do,
brother Jim, three years her senior, breaks into a grin.
"What have we here? A new movie star?"

Or a boy friend calls for her for a very special date, and
six-year-old Tommy, who has been flattening himself be-

47

hind the living-room door, jumps out at him with a wild shriek, "Hands up, horse stealer, or I shoot!"

It's easy to say that a sense of humor will see you through occasions like these. But if you are still a little insecure in your grown-up status, such teasing is apt to bring you closer to tears than to laughter. It does not help if Dad joins Jim in poking a bit of fun at you, or Mother defends Tommy by saying, "He was only playing!"

In your struggle for self-esteem, sometimes you are convinced that Dad is in close cahoots with Jim in wanting to keep you a baby, and that Mother loves Tommy more than she does you, and lets him get away with anything. And if you dare to lash out in a fit of temper at your tormentors, both parents are sure to turn their disapproval on you.

The larger the family, the bigger the problem often becomes. Anna Marie, fifteen, in frank despair, described her siblings as "nasty little pests" who set up a circus every time she tried asking girl and boy friends to the house. "All the same, Mom and Dad expect me to be the babysitter if they go out, and to do all kinds of chores around the house that my younger sister slides out of easily. They just don't love me as they do the others!"

Shirley is a junior in high school and wants to go on to college. The eldest of a family of six children, she knows she must win a scholarship, as her parents do not have the means to send her. For this, she must make good grades. But how can she study? Their house is small. She shares a room with two younger sisters, nine and five, who play and sometimes quarrel loudly at her elbow when she sits down to do homework. Or, if she waits till a little later, the TV blasts a "western" through the place, as her brothers turn to their favorite diversion.

Sheila, seventeen, also shares a room with her sister

Martha, fourteen. Her parents have accorded their elder daughter many privileges in keeping with her age, but which Martha, quite understandably, resents. They are strict about Martha's bedtime, but not about hers. Sheila has a larger allowance, and is trusted to choose her own clothes. She can stay out late at a party. She has a boy friend she regards as her "steady."

The situation is hard for Martha—and hard for Sheila too. Martha feels cheated because Sheila has so much more than she. Sheila is naturally frustrated when she looks for the blouse she meant to wear on a date and finds Martha not only borrowed it but got it badly soiled and stained. Sheila tries to be generous, but she loves nice things—and the drawers in the tall chest she shares are constantly in a whirling mess, as Martha ransacks them for a scarf, a pair of nylons, a piece of costume jewelry she fancies. "Just a loan," she explains glibly if Sheila objects. "Don't be stingy—you're not wearing it today."

Yes, poor Martha is reacting to her sense of privation—and Sheila is becoming more and more put out with her. The climax came recently when Martha went into the drawer of Sheila's worktable, took out a letter Bill had written her, and aired its contents to youngsters up and down the street. Bill learned about it and was very huffy. Martha was punished—but the harm was done.

Siblings—brothers and sisters, both younger and older—can be the cause of many heartaches during your adolescence. That is true, no matter how much affection you have for them.

What to do about it? Well, first of all, let's consider attitudes. You are seeking maturity. The mature person knows that frustrations of many kinds will be his lot throughout life. So he learns to handle them with a certain amount of calm, rather than waste his nervous energy on emotional explosions.

But that does not mean that he fails to seek solutions to the problems that eternally arise. Calmly, he analyzes the essential elements of the difficulty, in order to seek a way out. Sometimes, in adult life, there is *no* way out, and the individual must bow his head to fate. That is seldom true with the problems of adolescence, and particularly those of sibling dissensions. They can usually be resolved by understanding and honest effort.

Get in mind that though you and your brothers and sisters belong to the same parents, you are very different individuals, each with a unique personality that is growing and developing in a somewhat different environment. Why different? Simply because each, by reason of his age, occupies a different place in the household. Your parents simply cannot treat you all *alike*—though they should treat you all fairly. If they grant *you* certain privileges because you are older, by the same token they rely on you to shoulder heavier responsibilities. Whether you are the eldest, in the middle, or somewhere down the line, accept the place where you are and the demands it makes on you. There is no partiality involved in treating children of various ages differently.

In your secret heart you probably love these brothers and sisters of yours, and you should understand that they love you too, even though at times they display jealousy, or indifference, or even selfishness. They have their inner discipline to work out too—and if yours is not perfect yet, how do you expect theirs to be? Martha's motive in taking her sister's blouse may have been a desire to imitate her by dressing up—a tinge of jealousy mingled with admiration. It is even likely she boasts about Sheila to her friends. Is it possible she did not see how unfair she was being in spreading the contents of Bill's letter, but was seeking to bask in the prestige of her older sister's more grown-up boy-girl relationship?

It is fairly natural that jealousies should occur in the relationships of children in a family. Each one wants to stand first in the affections of Mother and Dad, and unconsciously resents having to move over and share the place with others. The little teasings and meannesses and squabbles are not always about the things they seem to be about, such as allowances or bedtime, or the program to be watched on TV. They are frequently outcroppings of the babyish desire to be the center of attention. But there is solidarity among siblings, too. The brothers who were battling a moment ago are apt to close ranks very quickly if the bully from the next block attacks one of them. If the girl who called her siblings little pests awoke and found the house afire while they were fast asleep in their beds, there is no doubt what she would do.

"I'm so glad I have younger brothers and sisters!" one girl who is a senior in high school exclaimed. "Sometimes they bother me—but I know they look up to me, and that's such a wonderful feeling. I have to bring home good reports so they won't be ashamed of me, and to set them a good example. It must be very sad to be an only child. It's such a good feeling to have others to love and to love you."

That girl had got hold of a very important tool in the solution of sibling difficulties: *leadership*. Sometimes it is yours to exert, if you are the eldest of the brood—or at least older than the one with whom the clashes occur. Sometimes it is yours to pass graciously to an older brother or sister, with the flattering suggestion that you are ready to talk things over and follow what he or she can offer as the best way out of trouble.

Take the case of the elder brother who teases his adolescent sister, who is just becoming conscious of personal appearance, or beginning to go out with boys. It's more than likely he dotes on her. He may have felt some resentment when she first arrived, and his mother had no more time to tie his shoe strings or admire his cunning little ways, because she had to take care of the new baby. But in time he came to love the darling little girl who pattered after him and looked up to him as a hero. He mended her toys and pulled her on her sled in winter, and taught her to ride a bicycle. He enjoyed the role of the all-knowing big brother.

But now, things have changed. The little sister is growing up and seeking independence. She's not so apt to rely on him as she used to be, and his teasing, though good-natured, may be his unconscious reaction to his loss of the hero role.

If she understood this, she might take it more lightly, instead of allowing it to create bad feelings. She might even, now and then, appeal to his big-brother leadership. "Walt, do you think this new hair-do is becoming?" "Walt, what should a girl talk about on a date with a boy—*you* ought to know!" "Walt, *you're* old enough to drive a car— maybe you'd drop me at Mary's house."

These little gestures of recognition that he is still the big brother won't lose her a single thing in her growing-up struggle—they may even gain her a valuable ally in her quest for new and special privileges. And she probably will discover that the teasing is no more.

In the case of Sheila and Martha, a frank, sisterly talk is certainly in order—but not an angry one. Here is Sheila's big opportunity to show her skill at leadership. Martha is old enough to understand that other people have their rights. Sheila should remind her that she tries to be generous and has often lent her a blouse, a belt, a scarf or bit of jewelry. But of course they should agree on what may be taken, for that is only fair. Sheila might ask Martha to help her decide which drawers in the big chest each is to have for her personal belongings, not to be invaded without permission by the other. She might suggest that each of them consider one corner of the room as her very own—and that they ask Dad to build a shelf and bulletin board in Martha's part, to house her scattered collection of knickknacks and pictures.

If Sheila can come to terms with Martha in a quiet, friendly way, she will have proved her adult status. If in spite of a good try, she should fail, then it will be time for a family conference. Not a tattletale session—but one in which rules of fair play are established with parental backing and, of course, with Martha present.

The family talk-it-over session is a cure for a great many troubles you may be experiencing. Try to choose a moment when Mother and Dad aren't tired and edgy, and make it something better than a complaint session. You might, for instance, suggest that your parents need a night out together occasionally, and that you will manage the home front if they will set the rules. Then you can bring up your own need to have friends in now and then, and not be interfered with by pranks that upset a pleasant get-together. Fairness and generosity—real love and understanding— are the oil that keeps family relationships running smoothly. Try pouring a little on troubled waters in your own home.

One girl demanded that she either be paid for baby-sitting her siblings when the parents went out, or be allowed to give a party for her friends the same night. Her father put his foot down on that. Such a plan could lead to all sorts of unfortunate happenings, and no parents could enjoy an evening of recreation fraught with worry about those they had left at home. It might seem reasonable to have a girl friend in to do homework or watch TV after the younger children were in bed—but the party plans should be held for another night.

Should you expect to be paid for home baby-sitting, if you have reached the age where outside baby-sitting is adding to your allowance? That is a matter you should weigh carefully. Are you doing a great many other chores that contribute to family well-being? Do your parents agree that baby-sitting, if it is frequently required, is something beyond the call of duty and deserves recompense? Some parents do feel that it is. But before you push the matter too strongly, measure your request for payment against all you may gain by a simple show of co-operation and generosity.

Everybody, at whatever age, needs some privacy. None more so than the high school student who must concentrate on homework. If the house is small, and the family large, it is often nearly hopeless to try to get a quiet hour for study.

But not entirely hopeless. Here is a matter that calls for consultation with your parents. They are sure to want you to do well at school, and will even make personal sacrifices to see that you have an hour of quiet privacy for study. If, like Sheila, you share a room with little sisters; if like her, you have brothers who keep the TV blasting while you need to work on your math problems, ask Mother and Dad to help you devise a schedule that will give you the necessary study time.

One father takes his two active little boys out and gives them handball practice before supper, while his teen-age daughter has a go at her lessons. A mother plays par-cheesi with the youngsters in the evening to keep their small apartment quiet during the study hour. If you plan to do your homework immediately on arriving home from school the younger children may be outdoors playing anyhow, and your mother, if consulted, will help to see that they do not come running in and out, shouting or quarreling to disturb you. Homework in crowded quarters takes planning. Do not be afraid to ask politely that a plan be made.

In our country we believe in and try to follow the standards we call "democracy." In their essence, they are just what you should be striving for in your home—fair play, respect for other personalities and for other people's needs, respect for yourself and for your needs too. There is a measure and a nice balance to be sought, an inner discipline to be attained, that are not required by people who live under a dictatorship and do what they are told. Such people remain always nearer the level of infancy.

Your home is a school of democracy, and the lessons you learn there will go with you throughout life. So, give it and yourself a break. Bring to it all of your best, in good humor and leadership and co-operation, and loving kindness, and politeness. In the wide world you will need these things, in order to prove fair to people much more unlike you, perhaps, than your brothers and sisters are. You may have to mingle and deal with people who have suffered many disadvantages, who have different religions, different nationality or racial backgrounds, different economic status than yourself. They, too, will be demanding fair play, respect for their personalities, help in resolving their problems, a chance to pursue happiness. The maturity you achieve among your brothers and sisters will be very useful in taking the measure of what you owe to other people with whom you come in contact throughout your life.

CHAPTER FIVE

SCHOOL DAYS

What is the best way to study?
Are math and social studies necessary for a girl?
*Will high school help me much if I don't expect to
   go on to college?*
*Are lessons all that matter? Shouldn't I have some
   fun in high school?*
Is it all right to choose electives that are easy?

Now that you are in high school your big job is to get as
much education as you can. Are you building up resources
that will contribute to your enjoyment of life and to your
life's work? Think of the high school years as a period when
you are gaining the maturity and understanding of yourself
and others that will enable you to live successfully in a
complex modern world.

At present approximately one-fifth of the high school
graduates in this country go on to higher education. For
this group, these four years are preparation for college—
but for *all* of you, they are preparation for living. Whether
you continue your studies in order to enter a profession,
find a job after graduation, or marry, you will be a more
interesting, more successful person if you take full advantage of all that high school offers. Make the most of
these four years to form friendships with girls and boys,

become acquainted with some of the vast store of knowledge that has come down through the ages, try out your own abilities, learn about yourself and your attitudes toward others, store up riches you can draw upon for future happiness.

There is one thing you ought to think about very early, and that is the proper planning of your high school curriculum. If you are one of a large family and the cost of a college education seems to make it an impossibility, don't give up the idea too quickly. Take the subjects required for college entrance. There are many avenues, which we will discuss later, open to the girl who is serious about this. You would not want to discover too late that the lack of a credit—say in science—meant that college was out for you. Consult your teacher or adviser and make out a program that meets college requirements.

If you are very certain that under no circumstances will you consider college, you might plan a program of practical business courses. But do include as many cultural subjects as you can fit in. Neither high school nor college will write *finis* to your education. These are the years in which to acquire a broad background of cultural interests from which you will go on to educate yourself. For, as one college president recently put it, that is what everyone must do, since no one can learn your lessons for you. And those we call "self-educated" men and women can acquire the knowledge of college graduates, if not the degrees.

Some girls miss out on part or all of their high school opportunities. Carol Jean could hardly wait for the day when she would get her diploma. She studied just enough to get by, took no real interest in the subjects on her program, nor in clubs or other activities, and would have wished away four years of her life—her high school years —if she could.

Gay, popular Sue could not bear to say "No." She was on so many committees, had so many parties and dates that she never had time to study. Her fun was often spoiled by the nagging feeling of work undone, and she almost flunked social studies before she realized that her lack of proportion in budgeting her time for fun, extracurricular activities and study was likely to mean her rejection by the college she dreamed of attending.

Alice was a quiet, shy girl who blushed when she was called on to recite. She hurried to her classes without speaking to any of her classmates, and rushed away again as if she had an important appointment to keep and her time were worth a fortune. She never joined any of the groups of girls who ate lunch together, never remained for any after-school events. And she positively shriveled up if a boy spoke to her.

Are you, like Alice, *missing all the fun and companionship of high school?* Take a hint from Debra. Her family had recently moved to town and she needed to make new boy and girl friends. She made up her mind to smile and say hello without waiting for others to speak to her first. She resolved to be friendly and helpful to the boys and girls in her various classes, and she planned to choose extracurricular activities that appealed to her and would put her in contact with boys and girls who shared her interests. She had a good voice and liked to act, so she joined the drama club and later the choir. She tried out for the tennis and volley ball teams because she enjoyed these sports. Thus she met congenial friends with whom, on special occasions at school and at home and school parties, she not only had good times, but gradually became more and more at ease in social situations.

Jane could not remain for after-school activities because she had to take the school bus from a consolidated high school. She was bashful and retiring because she felt that the town girls were more sophisticated and better dressed than she. At home she was expected to do a great many chores because she was the eldest in a large family. She did not try very hard to master her lessons at school because they seemed to her to have so little connection with her life.

Really, Jane could learn a great deal in high school that would enrich her life and make it happier. Part of the task of making friends is up to the other girls, of course, but much of it rests with her. She might ask their advice in learning to dress better and in social skills that are unfamiliar to her. She might talk to her teacher about some way to remain in town occasionally—perhaps overnight with one of the girls—so that she could share in the after-school activities and good times. She might try to plan with her mother so as to have more time for her studies and a chance to profit by high school social life.

One of the important things about learning is the incentive, the desire. Bright boys and girls are sometimes indifferent or downright poor students until their interest is aroused. Once they have the wish to learn, studying comes easy. Perhaps when Jane is one of the crowd, her studies will have meaning in her life and her lessons will show it.

Do you, like Carol Jean, *work only enough to get by?* Do you think of high school as a series of disconnected, uninteresting courses that you must pass to win the freedom of a diploma? Stop a minute and think what these required subjects can mean in your life. Take English literature and grammar. No matter what your future, you will need to communicate with others. The truly effective adult expresses himself readily and well, has a background of culture, and finds pleasure in good books. The books you read in high school give you a taste for good books and standards by which to measure even "best sellers." All this makes you a more attractive person to know, a more interesting wife and mother.

How about Social Studies, or Citizenship Education? There is fascination in learning all you can about your country and the world you live in. To function successfully in the present, to be a worthwhile citizen of our democracy, you will need to know all you can about its past and present; and the physical, economic and political aspects of other countries with which we must deal. How else can you exercise your privileges and fulfill your duties as a good citizen?

Do you think of your language classes as a means of broadening and enriching your personality? Many Americans expect the other fellow to speak English, and he usually does. In the large cities and metropolitan hotels around the world English is spoken. But how much a traveler misses if he cannot speak the language of the country! Even if you never go abroad, there are many opportunities to speak foreign languages right here at home. We can understand people of other countries and backgrounds better if we are able to read their books and speak their language. As the countries of the world draw closer together in such organizations as the United Nations, the need for understanding increases.

When you are earning your own living, or are the mistress of your own household, how will you "get your money's worth," manage your salary, figure your income tax, carry on a thousand and one matters of daily life, if you never learn to think mathematically?

What about the value of electives? Aren't you wasting your opportunities if you choose courses just because they are reputed to be "snaps," or the instructor has a reputation for being easy? Home Economics teaches in addition to cooking and sewing and home decoration, such important things as family relations—the whole science of conducting a home and caring for children. Music, Art, Dramatics offer big dividends in resources for leisure time all your life.

Do you, like Sue, *become so involved in social and extra-curricular activities that you have little time for study?* Then perhaps you need to stop and give some thought to *why* you are in school, to learn to budget your time and to study more effectively.

A hundred years ago only a small group of young people went to high school. Today 85 per cent of boys and girls between the ages of fourteen and seventeen are enrolled in secondary schools. By 1965 it is expected that there will be over thirteen million high school students. Everyone has come to see that a democracy like ours needs citizens who have been properly trained to take responsibility; who have good vocational skills; good habits of work and health; know how to use their leisure time in creative ways; can go on to establish good homes and pass on to their children helpful attitudes toward all other citizens.

Stop and ask yourself how well you are profiting by these things which your community is spending so much money to give you. Will you be able to fulfill your responsibility as a citizen, not merely as a voter and taxpayer, but as an intelligent, well-informed, active member of your community and of your country? Will you have the training to earn an adequate living? To be a good homemaker?

A home is the smallest unit of a democracy—a place where your children will need you to teach them how to work and play together. Will you measure up to your role as a mother? You will if you are now learning to know yourself and get along with others; mastering skills that are useful in the home, such as sewing, cooking, child and health care; learning how to lead and how to follow; how to enjoy good music, books, hobbies; how to make the most of all high school has to offer in the development of your personality. We hope you won't be like Carol Jean who said, "I wasted four years of my life, and now I can never get them back!"

Sarah was interested in several hobbies and liked good times, but she wanted to make good grades, too. In order to have as much time for fun and out-of-class interests as she could, she determined to get as much as possible out of each minute invested in study. She made up her mind to start every new subject with each day's homework as perfect as she could make it. If she understood a subject in the beginning of the term, she knew she would be less likely to have difficulty later on. If she did not get it at first, she was likely to be more and more confused all term. She never hesitated to ask questions of her teachers, either in class or after hours, when she did not understand a point in the day's lesson or last night's homework. She realized the value of establishing an early reputation as a conscientious, interested student, and she found that paying strict attention in class made her homework easier and cut down on the time she needed to spend on it.

Sarah chose a time—seven-thirty to nine-thirty each evening—that suited her best to study, and allowed only the most unusual circumstances to interfere with it, because she knew that if she permitted constant exceptions her whole plan might fall through. She arranged to do her studying each night in her own room where she would have quiet and be undisturbed. She asked her mother to take any calls she received during that time and to say she would call back later. She used a wide desk table under a good light that fell over her left shoulder. She kept a dictionary and an atlas handy and used them frequently.

When she needed to use an encyclopedia or other reference books she stopped at the library and got that over with on her way home.

Before she began to study, she made a point of thinking over what the lesson was about and recalling all she had heard about it in class. She looked over any charts, chapter headings or notes she had previously made. While she studied she read as fast as she could, sending whole sentences or ideas to her brain as she did when she read an exciting whodunit. She was stern about wandering attention or any waste of time daydreaming. She stopped to repeat in her own words each paragraph she read, and at the end of her study period she jotted down the main points of what she had learned.

Sarah found she accomplished more if she used her study periods at school for the subjects on which she found it easiest to concentrate with others around, and she made every minute count, as she did in her home study periods. Her grades were always high but, best of all, she had plenty of time for her extracurricular interests.

Maybe you need to take a leaf out of Sarah's book and learn to study more efficiently and more effectively. You may have to adapt her program a bit. Possibly you do not have a quiet room of your own in which to study. Maybe you do not have two free hours from seven-thirty to nine-thirty in the evening. Modify Sarah's program to suit your circumstances, but give her system a tryout. You may find it pays off in higher marks and a lot more leisure than you have ever had before.

Your high school years should be happy ones—exciting first dates, the sharp, tangy smell of a chrysanthemum corsage while you cheer your head off for the football hero, slumber parties and all-girl gab fests when you discuss LIFE and LOVE and everything else under the sun, silly jokes and laughter with the crowd at the after-school hang-out, the enchantment of music, formal gowns, soft lights and gay decorations at proms.

They should also be the years when you make great strides toward becoming the person you hope to be; when you grow in knowledge and ability; explore your aptitudes; become acquainted with what has been thought and done in the world; develop attitudes that will help you to live successfully and make some contribution of your own, however small, to society.

It's up to you. Now you are grown-up enough to begin to manage your own life, make your own choices, attend to your own discipline. Will you be Alice, Carol Jean, Sue, Debra, or Sarah? This is a choice you must make for yourself. Mom and Dad, your teachers, your friends can help, but they cannot do it for you. Only you can make your high school years a happy, successful time.

CHAPTER SIX

YOUR GIRL FRIENDS

*How should I act if other girls seem jealous of my
   popularity?*
*Can I keep my friends if I cross them in the things
   they want to do?*
Will high averages make me unpopular?
*What can I do if my best friend suddenly turns
   against me?*
*How can I make new friends after being uprooted
   from my home town or from my old school?*

When girls are asked what they desire most, they often
reply: "I want to be popular." And they don't just mean
with boys—though of course that is something with which
a girl is beginning to be concerned during the teen years.
They mean with both boys and girls, especially those their
own age they meet at school.

How can I be more popular with my classmates? By
having a bigger allowance to spend? By wearing smarter
clothes? By throwing a big party? By acting like Eloise,
who is always taking over and running things?

Recently Eloise learned a big lesson about popularity:
you can hold the center of the stage too long! She has
excellent qualities of leadership, is full of original ideas, and
often feels that plans would slump if she didn't give them

a push in the right direction. For a long time, everyone seemed to agree with her. Last year she was class president, had the lead in the class play, was elected to a number of important posts. This year everything changed, to her confusion and chagrin. She lost out in the various elections to young people she could not help regarding as less capable than herself. Boys and girls still laughed at her wisecracks and seemed to enjoy her vivacity—but when the vote was cast for "most popular girl," quiet, serious-minded Elizabeth was chosen. Why? When the casting for roles in the play took place, the dramatic teacher assigned her a part with only a few lines, although surely everyone recognized that she was a clever little actress.

These setbacks cut Eloise to the heart. "What have I done," she asked, "that everyone has turned against me? I'm the same girl as last year! What have I *done* that nobody likes me?"

Her nearest and dearest girl friend gave her the answer. "You haven't done anything, Eloise," she said. "And it isn't true that nobody likes you. But—well, I guess they want to see if you can be a good sport and take a back seat for awhile, and give some of the others a chance at the spotlight."

"But I worked hard at the jobs they gave me—and even the town newspaper said I was wonderful in the play. It isn't fair to cut me out of everything!"

"Yes, it's fair. I'm your friend, and I think it's fair. You just had too much success last year—and it can build up jealousies. You know what you should do if you want to stay popular?"

"No—and I feel so bad I hardly care."

"I'll tell you anyhow. Go congratulate the new class president and the 'most popular' girl, and the one who has the lead in the play. And *mean* it, too. You'll see what it will do for you."

Eloise had a hard fight with her pride—but in the end, the friendship of her classmates meant so much to her she decided to take the advice. Maybe it cost her more than anyone knew to tell those who had won out over her how happy she was for them. Maybe she did not *quite mean it,* until she saw their reactions of surprise and delight. The boy she most admired caught hold of her in the hall and exclaimed, "Eloise, I wasn't sure you had it in you! You're the nicest little sport I ever heard about!" And she knew she had learned a lesson and won a reward.

This year she is happier than ever. She is not finding the back seat lonely, for it always seems to be surrounded by young people who ask her advice and praise her for her helpfulness. But she's given up trying to run everything. She's even discovered that plenty of other people have good ideas.

Sonia has a different sort of popularity problem. She is very conscientious in her studies—and especially fond of math. She always makes high marks. Her dream has been to become a scientist, and it's more than likely she could make it.

Lately, though, the math teacher has been noticing her long face, and a certain hesitancy when he called on her to recite. She acted as if something was terribly wrong, and he decided to ask her. Was she ill? Was there trouble at home?

No, nothing like that. After much persuasion, Sonia gave the true answer. "It's great to be good at math, and I do love it! But I guess the others all hate me because they think I'm too smart. Lately they've even nicknamed me 'the brain.' Jean made up her party list in the lunchroom right in front of me—and left me out! I just can't bear it. If I want to have friends, I have to be dumb."

In a day when brains are so much needed in the world, it's too bad for a girl like Sonia to have to be ashamed of hers. But her problem was a real one—harder to solve, perhaps, than any in algebra. The math teacher was puzzled. He stared at Sonia, sitting there with tears coursing down her cheeks, more eager for friendship than for good marks. Then he had a bright idea. "See here, Sonia," he said, "there's a way out of your dilemma. You know, some of your classmates *do* find algebra and geometry awfully hard. Why don't you offer to help them? I'm not suggesting you pass around your homework for the others to copy. But helping isn't cheating, you know. I can mention a few girls who could profit by your co-operation. Why don't you offer to get together with them for homework, after school or at study hour? They might be grateful."

Sonia already has made the offer, and is delighted with the way it is working out. Ann Norbeck not only asked her over to her house to study; she invited her to a Saturday night square dance she's having in their basement recreation room. "It's a good chance for you to get in with our bunch, Sonia," she said. "I'm sorry, we all thought you were stuck-up and mean. I think you're just great!"

Yes, friendships are a "must," in any girl's life. The price of them is not flashier clothes, nor more money to spend, but more understanding of others, more give-and-take. You pay for friendship with friendliness. Sonia is already more sympathetic with those who have trouble working math problems—and they are showing a readiness to help her with *her* problem. Here is something that can grow into a lifetime of happiness.

When you entered high school you came in contact, for the first time perhaps, with boys and girls from distant neighborhoods, who often lived quite differently. Some might have parents who were foreign-born, with ideas that seemed strange to you about how their daughters should behave. Some were from homes of greater luxury than yours; while with others it was just the reverse.

No wonder that in this new setting you were a bit bewildered. You were eager to fit in and be accepted, but a little unsure of yourself. Finally, though, it happened: another girl smiled at you and said, "Hi!" You smiled back and answered her greeting. Now the strangeness would wear off. Happily, you were no longer alone.

Very soon, in fact, you found yourself a member of a small clique, or bunch—your bunch of girls who liked to run around together. You had enough tastes in common to get along, enough get-up-and-go to start the ball rolling toward good times. *Your* bunch became your little island of safety in a bigger ocean than you had ever tried to swim in, up to now. Because your new friends liked you and wanted you, you took a big jump in self-confidence. Your feeling of loyalty made you accept their judgment about a great many things in preference to that of your parents. If they decreed lipstick, or a later curfew, or any other thing, you felt you must conform. Like you, they were becoming interested in boys. Like you, they were growing up physically and mentally, and wanting to make their own set of rules to take the place of home discipline and controls. They gave you the very courage you needed to start being yourself.

Should you always follow what the bunch does or wants to do? Well, yes and no. Maybe this is where your chance comes to show that you can both lead and follow. Eloise was a good leader—but she had to learn to follow too. Yet a wishy-washy girl who always meekly follows other people's say-so is in almost as much danger as Eloise of losing rather than cementing friendships. If your bunch are the right sort of girls, they will respect you and like you better if you sometimes say "No" to a plan or project —particularly if it violates your own high standards. Here is where good leadership comes in. Help *make* the rules and you'll find it easier to conform to them.

What about a best friend? Many girls say they need not only friends, but also one "best friend." Very likely you know such a girl. She is the member of your bunch who is most like you in every way, and with whom you share confidences. Certainly you could never tell *all* your thoughts to a boy friend, no matter how much you thought of him. Your really, truly "best friend," who is passing through the same experiences as you, is the answer to your need.

You and your best friend may share homework time and hobbies, as well as hopes and dreams. Maybe you two have turned to sewing, and are making some new, glamorous clothes. Or you may get together and experiment on hairdos. She is the only one who knows about your crush on a particular boy who as yet has paid no attention to you— and perhaps she can offer some advice, or even help by inviting him to her house with a few others, so it won't be too obvious. She cheers and comforts you, and you can't imagine ever giving her up.

A best friend is a wonderful asset, at any time in life, and particularly in the teen years. But things do happen to cause a drawing apart, even of the best of friends.

There is, for instance, the green monster, jealousy. The very boy for whom Mabel has confided her admiration takes a shine to you instead, and invites you to the school dance. You feel that perhaps you ought to turn him down, but you haven't the courage, because it might mean staying home. So you go with him—but after that a chill descends on your girl-to-girl relationship. Mabel says she doesn't care a bit—

aren't there plenty of boys she can have?—but you know her trust in your loyalty has been shaken.

Sandra and Jean were so inseparable the bunch named them "the twins." They were buddies in everything— swimming, sewing, skating, cooking. When they'd been apart less than an hour, they found things to confide by telephone. Then they both entered party dresses they had made in the fashion show their bunch had promoted at school—and Sandra's won first award. Jean honestly felt that hers was the prettiest and the best sewing. She was hurt more than she cared to admit. Their friendship teetered for a whole week. Then Sandra went to her and said, "Jean, we're not rivals, we're friends. I'm sorry I won if it hurt your feelings, but I didn't do anything to stack the cards. If the next time you win, I'll try to be a good sport."

Sandra was wise to talk things out frankly with Jean, who had to admit that she was being unfair. And so the breach in their friendship was quickly healed.

If your best friend and you are members of a larger group, things are sure to go better between you. Elsa and Sally did not go with a gang. They always just clung together. They had no need for anyone but themselves. It was a perfect friendship—or so it seemed. They did homework together, went on hikes together, sometimes were allowed to stay overnight at one or the other's house.

But perhaps it was not all quite perfect. Sally got a little restless. Sometimes she had the feeling that Elsa's was the stronger personality, and that she was becoming just a rubber stamp. Then a new girl came to their high school. She acted lonely and disoriented, and Sally generously took her in tow at lunchtime. They discovered they both had a keen interest in water-color sketching, and the next Saturday afternoon they went on a hike together with their painting equipment. Sally asked Elsa to come along —but Elsa huffily refused. She was furious at the new girl, who deliberately had "stolen" her best friend.

A cold wave from the North Pole came between Elsa and Sally. Secretly, Elsa shed bitter tears. Her loss left her totally forsaken, with no one to care about her horrible loneliness.

Then one afternoon after school, Sally insisted on taking her arm and walking along with her. "Elsa," she said, "you know I'm your friend. But why can't we have other friends too? That new girl is interesting, and so are a lot of others we ought to be getting to know. I want you for my friend, but I don't want to live in a cage any more. I think we ought to move out and have more social life."

Elsa was tired of sulking—and hungry for the old friendship. But she had to agree it should never be a strict twosome again. Later she was so glad she did. She and Sally became the center of a group that shared many interests and had many good times. The new girl—well, she wasn't "new" after that, although she did have many good slants and fun ideas she had brought from her old school.

Sometimes an even more difficult situation comes between two girls who have been best friends. Greta and Molly were inseparable for two whole years. The friendship had started in seventh grade, and continued into junior high. They lived fairly near each other, and that made matters easier.

Greta simply could not understand what happened. They had had no quarrel or difference of any kind. Yet Molly began giving her the brush-off. If Greta went over to her house, Molly always has some excuse for getting rid of her —a headache, an errand or chore. At school, Molly would pass Greta with a quick "Hi!" and appear embarrassed and annoyed if Greta pursued her. What was wrong? What *could* be wrong?

Nothing, perhaps, that Greta could do much about for the moment. Perhaps later these two old friends might find each other again. They were the same age, had many tastes in common. But Molly was maturing faster than Greta physically. Molly had reached the menarche, and Greta as yet had not. Molly was growing up, feeling herself a young lady, dreaming of boy friends and dates. Greta was still at the "little girl" stage in looks and in feelings—and Molly found it embarrassing to have her tagging along.

It was hard, very hard for Greta. If she had understood better, she might have borne her loss more easily. In a year or two, perhaps in a matter of months, she would be catching up with Molly. It's true, they might both have made new close friends by then. But the old liking for each other need not be wholly wiped out. It might even cast a warm glow over a more mature friendship.

When we were talking about that new girl who came to Elsa's school, you may have reflected on how difficult it is to put down roots in the wider friendships of adolescence —and then to be suddenly uprooted and torn away from your best friend and your gang and everything you know best—and plopped down in strange territory where other young people are well-acquainted and having fun together, and you are the outsider.

Only during the great migrations of ancient history have families been on the move as they are in America today, as a result of industrial changes and military necessity. And so, young people must be prepared for the adjustments that inevitably face them in such circumstances.

New girl in town. What is the best course for a girl in this situation? For, unless she can quickly acquire a whole new set of friends, often in some bewildering new environment, her teen years are apt to be as arid as the Sahara.

We know of one girl who was just making plans for her junior prom in a large high school in Alabama, when her father, an Air Force colonel, was shifted to Labrador. It was a shock, of course—and besides, when she reached that far-off land of snow, there was only one other American girl her age on the entire post. "How nice," she exclaimed later, "that we liked each other!"

You can guess that with that attitude she adjusted readily to the new, strange setting. When she entered the tiny country school across the line in Canada for her senior high school year, she discovered at once that she also liked the Canadian young people, and could enjoy the simple good times they had. She liked the Eskimos she met, and found there were things she could learn from them.

This girl took along with her a fund of friendliness that would make her accepted anywhere. Naturally, she had some heartaches for the old comrades—but she refused to dwell on them. She was mature enough not to allow herself to be frustrated by the unexpected upheaval in her life.

Often there is so much fear—or resentment—in the up-rooted one's heart that she fails to make the effort to fit in. She may look with scorn on the young people she finds in the new environment. Their school may be overcrowded and out-of-date; their pastimes appear silly. She lets her thoughts dwell on the past—finds no relish in the new adventure. And, as she withdraws into her shell, those who might have been her friends mark her down for a hopeless prig.

The price of friendship is friendliness. That goes especially for the making of new friends. If your family migrates, and you must go along, remember that. Your attitude is the important thing. Find out all that is going on in the new place and how you can fit in and maybe be useful. Are you good at wielding a paintbrush on stage scenery? Then you might help with decorations for the play. You were rehearsing for the lead at your old school? Don't so much as whisper it! Here, as a humble stagehand you will have your chance to acquire friends.

Sharing skills is always a good way to make and keep friends, no matter where you are. Do you have a hobby— knitting, sewing, painting, tap or ballet dancing, stamp collecting, bird watching? Let others in on your enthusiasm, and show them how the thing is done. It's one sure road to popularity. Everyone likes to learn a new trick that can be fun.

A sense of humor helps with friendships, too. That is, provided it's the right sense of humor. The girl who can laugh at herself, who can laugh *with* others but never *at* others, will have many happy relationships. The girl who gossips about other girls—but, don't let's dwell on her! She is very immature, and probably has few friends.

Stop and rate yourself on warmth of friendliness to all sorts of people; on readiness to lead and willingness to follow; on sharing—of things and friendships and good times and skills; on your ability to meet big or small frustrations and disappointments with cheerfulness.

When you have done that, you will have some notion of how many real friends you possess, and how much satisfaction is in store for you.

CHAPTER SEVEN

YOUR BOY FRIENDS

What sort of girl do boys like?
How can I get a boy I like interested in me?
Is it all right to go on a blind date?
Should I kiss my date good night?—ask him in?
Must a girl pet to be popular?
Is going steady a good idea? How do I break off
with a steady?

You were barely twelve at the time. Your mother had
called twice to say that it was past time for you to be in
bed, but you lingered on the terrace. The moonlight was
so strong that you could almost see colors in the back
garden bed. You were dreaming. You still remember that
dream. You were pretty, poised, confident, laughing with
the crowd of handsome boys gathered around you. You
chose the tallest—

Now that you are older, your dream seems as unrealistic
as a fairy tale. You know you aren't poised and confident,
and you don't think you're pretty. Boys do not surround
you in droves. Like most girls from Maine to California
and back to Florida, you are full of questions about dating.
"How can I convince my parents I am old enough to date?"
"How can I become friends with boys without appearing to

to chase them?" "What kind of girl do boys like?" "Is it all right to telephone a boy?" "What about blind dates?"

Many of these questions cannot be answered in a word. There's a great difference in the ages at which young people begin to date. In some parts of the country they may go to movies, picnics, family parties, school affairs with boys while still in elementary school. In other places, dating begins well along in high school. Some parents are anxious to advance their daughter's social life, arranging dancing lessons, planning the first boy-and-girl parties. Other parents try to put the dating off as long as possible. If you had older brothers and sisters who paved the way for you, very likely you were allowed to date early.

Many schools give boys and girls an opportunity to meet socially through programs of extracurricular activities— drama groups, hobby clubs, dancing. Some communities have teen-age centers, active church youth organizations, neighborhood get-togethers, square dances, and other good times which help boys and girls to get to know each other in the more adult social way that you call dating. If there is nothing of this sort in your town, why not talk the matter over with some of the grownups connected with your school or church or local government? Perhaps you can get some such thing started.

We have seen that physical maturity comes to different girls at different ages. The girl who matures early is ready for dating before the one who has not yet reached the menarche. Girls in general mature earlier than boys and this causes complications for them in early dating. The girls try to get the boys interested in dancing parties and the boys complain that the girls pursue them. What is a girl to do? She may have to take the lead, but she will need to use tact. Not long ago she looked on boys with scorn, now they seem altogether different—exciting and strange—and she wants them to pay attention to her. How can she meet boys in this new relationship?

For Kate it was easy and natural. She had an older brother whose friends ran in and out of her house like members of the family. Even when Kate outgrew her little girl indifference and began to find them interesting as date material, she thought of them without awe or shyness and treated her brother's companions, the sons of family friends, the boys in her classes and clubs with a natural friendliness that insured her popularity.

"But what of me?" Ellen asks. "I'm an only child. And we've just moved to a new town where I don't know a soul."

There are many girls like Ellen in this country, where sociologists tell us the population is increasingly on the move. Even for them it should not be too difficult. They have the glamour of the new and unknown. If they are natural and outgoing, they are bound to make friends, including boy friends.

If you are a new girl in school or in town, don't dwell on your old town or make unfavorable comparisons with the new. Act as if you like life in your new community and want to be a part of it. Be friendly to the girls in your class and at your church. Girls have brothers and cousins to introduce to you. Don't push yourself forward, but at the same time, don't hang back. No boy is going to think you are chasing him because you say hello and take a friendly interest in him. Don't be one of those silly girls who snub boys and miss out on all the fun because they are afraid to show any normal liking for a boy. Did you ever think this might be a form of self-consciousness you ought to do something about in a hurry, if you want to be popular? Remember boys are often shy too, and as inexperienced as you are. They appreciate encouragement when a girl is not forward or does not behave like Diana on the hunt.

"What about using the telephone to make friends with a boy?" "Would it be all right to call a boy you are interested in on some such pretext as asking about tomorrow's algebra?" No, boys are jealous of their masculine prerogative of taking the initiative. They see through pretexts, and are apt to turn thumbs down on the girl who seems to be using the telephone as a weapon in her boy chasing. If her telephone calls subject them to teasing, they will see red.

There are occasions when it is necessary to telephone a boy, as for instance to give him an important message or invite him to a party. Give your name, ask for him, and when he comes to the phone make your call as brief as possible. And—don't let that sort of thing happen often.

What kind of girl do boys like? The Girl Scout magazine, *The American Girl*, put this query to high school boys across the country. They expressed some very definite views. They agreed that personality had it all over mere looks. It made little difference to them whether a girl was blond or redhead, short or tall, plump or thin, provided she had a friendly smile and was fun to be with. Rejecting tomboys, they held out for femininity. Good grooming— neatness, shining cleanliness of skin and hair, all the attributes that go to make up the "bandbox look"—ranked high on their lists of things they admired. Most boys approved the careful use of lipstick, but all of them vetoed heavy make-up. One boy wrote: "Clown make-up, mascara, long painted fingernails scare me." "When we double-date," wrote another, "I like my girl to pay attention to me and not the other fellow." "No fellow likes a show-off," still another declared. "The girl who always has to be the life of the party, and let everyone know she's around, giggling and talking to attract attention, makes me squirm. And nothing burns up a guy like having a girl call him away from his gang, letting him in for their kidding because she wants the world to know he belongs to her."

"I can't stand blasé females," Jim wrote. "I always fall for the girl who seems unconscious of herself because she seems to be having such a good time no matter what we're doing. I can't resist a girl who is lively and can hold her own in any conversation. She doesn't really have to be pretty if she has an air of confidence in her own charm."

There you have it. Boys admire girls who are feminine, well-groomed, friendly, and more interested in others than in themselves. They like to be with girls who are agreeable companions, who do not embarrass them with possessive airs, and who are at ease in social situations.

Jim admired the girl who could hold her own in conversation. Perhaps, like Midge, you have made a definite effort to acquire this skill. Midge liked to read and to draw. She spent a good deal of time by herself. She dreaded attending the class party because she knew she would be an uneasy wallflower. "Midge, this is Stanley Steward," said one of the chaperons, and walked off, leaving Midge blushing a burning crimson, alone with a strange boy.

What would you have done in Midge's place? Mumbled something and fled? You have no trouble talking to your girl friends. Your family are callous in their pleas for a respite from your chatter at home. But at your first parties, when a strange boy is introduced to you, you can't think of a word to say. Take a breath, relax, you can't think when you're tense. Boys are flesh-and-blood people, not so vastly different from other humans. Like everyone else, they are interested in themselves. Talk to them as you would to your girl friends. Ask them what games they play. What do they think of the local ball team? What are they going to do this vacation? When they answer, listen. Think of the conversation as a game of badminton. Keep the cock of conversation shuttling back and forth and never let it drop into the net. "I'm going to work at a summer camp in Danville," he says in answer to your question. "Danville," you repeat. "Where's that?" And so you continue tossing the cock to him until you have him telling you all about himself. Later, when you know him better, you won't grow panicky over occasional silences.

What about a line? Does a girl have to have a line to be popular? Not if you mean insincere patter meant to flatter the male ego. "Oh, Bill," Mary sighs, rolling her eyes, "you're *sooo* tall, poor little me has to bend way back —like this—" Boys soon discount all this and rate the girl as a silly lightweight. Compliments embarrass them. Baby talk is likely to disgust them.

If conversation comes hard with you, it's a good idea to run over a mental list of things to talk about in advance of a date—bits from the day's news, ball scores, team ratings, a funny cartoon you saw in *Life*. Of course, the give and take should be spontaneous to be fun, but it does no harm to have something in reserve to fill a slump, especially if the topic is in line with the interests of your date or the crowd.

You are of course the girl who resists all temptation to fill in a pause with catty remarks about other girls, or to entertain the crowd with choice bits of gossip. Boys find gossip and sniping at other girls distasteful.

How do you reply when a boy "hands you a line?" Do you stammer and blush? Do you squelch the boy efficiently to show how smart you are in recognizing it for what it is? It's better to play along, laugh and pay him back in the same coin. Gay banter is part of the lightness and fun of first dates. You'll progress to the sincerity of real friendship later with the boys who really interest you.

What do you do when the wrong boy calls? The problems of boy-girl relationships do seem endless. Here you have become friends with several boys and one of them calls you up to ask for a date. But he is not the one you like best. No matter, you will have to speak up with an answer of some kind. You won't raise your popularity rating by trying to hedge in case your favorite calls later. If you accept, do it without gushing, but in a way that shows you are happy to go with the boy. It is a good idea to repeat the time and place to make sure that arrangements are understood. If you refuse, do so at once with whatever explanation seems necessary. "I'm sorry, Bill, I have a date," or "I'll be out of town that night," or just plain, "I can't this time, Bill." If you already have a date and you are especially disappointed to have to refuse, do not hesitate to show it by adding, "Try me again, won't you, Bill?" If for some good reason you really are uncertain, explain the situation and tell the boy when he may expect an answer.

What do you do when that seemingly unattainable Jim you've been dreaming about calls up and asks to take you to the party, when you've just promised to go with good old reliable George? Better accept it as one of those exasperating tricks fate loves to play. Tell Jim how sorry you are and ask him to try you again. You know you'd regret it if you stood up George. It would be a shabby trick that would make you uncomfortable. Nor would it be likely to raise your stock with Jim or the other boys, when it got around as these things do.

If you are the one who suffers the humiliation of being all dressed up and ready for the date that doesn't show up, give the boy a chance to apologize and explain. There may be a very good reason why he failed to appear. Of course if he isn't gentleman enough to get in touch with you immediately, or his explanations are suspect, cross him off your list with thanks that you have discovered what he is really like.

Blind dates? A college freshman who had been popular throughout her high school years has this to say: "Blind dates can be boring or downright unpleasant unless they are arranged by friends who know you well enough to be sure your date will be someone congenial. I always make sure we are going to do something or go somewhere I know all about. I never take chances on strange places with strange dates. I don't expect Mr. Unknown to be Tod Hunter or Rock Hudson. But one of the boys I met that way, a shy, rather homely boy, has become a good friend."

"I've met boys I liked on blind dates," Julie said. "Do you think it would be all right for me to go out with a boy I met this afternoon on the beach?"

That is a little different. The strange date you pick up can be a pretty grave risk. There is no one to vouch for him, and you know nothing about his background. Boys and men often appear charmingly different on short acquaintance from what they really are. Then too, you must admit your experience as a judge of male character is limited. At best, if the stranger is a new boy in town, you may run the risk of appearing to him to be an easy pickup. At worst, you can court the hazard of becoming involved with a person who is undesirable or dangerous.

There's risk too in writing to boys you haven't met. If you and your family know and trust the person who puts you in touch with the boy, there's no reason why you shouldn't write to him if you want to. Of course, not having met him, you won't go in for intimate revelations in your letters. Be impersonal and entertaining and you will have no cause for embarrassment later on.

Unless you have some reliable guarantee of the kind of person the boy may be, it's wiser not to take him on as a pen pal. Distance can lend such enchantment in letters that there could be little fact and all fiction in the things he writes. The safety you count on in the miles that separate you can be rudely shattered when suddenly there appears on your doorstep a boy who may be embarrassingly different from what you expect him to be.

Perhaps you are walking down Main Street, a little self-consciously because you know that your new blue dress is mighty becoming. Ahead you see a group of boys from your school standing in front of the drugstore. You will have to pass right by them in a moment or two. Your heart jumps and you feel even more self-conscious. You make up your mind that you are not going to blush and look embarrassed. You have read that boys who are not yet quite grown-up enough to know how to treat girls often gang together and whistle or call out to show their pals they are aware of girls. Sure enough, they whistle as you approach, but you take a breath and stick to your resolution. You don't treat the whistle with icy disdain as if you were an insulted Queen Victoria. You don't encourage the boys in this behavior by tossing out a wisecrack to make them laugh. You look at them, smile in a friendly fashion, and continue on your way. The girl who is outraged, acts scared or kittenish or fresh, makes a bad impression, but a boy's interest may be aroused by a girl who appears approachable and friendly as she goes her way. Comments, wolf whistles from strange boys or older men should be quietly ignored.

First dates. Usually first dates are invitations to some specific function—a party, game, play, or school or church affair. What to do for the evening is not your responsibility. But if a boy calls up and asks for a date on a Saturday night when there is nothing going on, what then? You might inquire tactfully whether he has anything in mind—the movies, bowling, skating—so that you can dress appropriately. Later when you have become friends and see each other more often, the fun you have together will be partly your concern. The more interesting and imaginative you are, the more successful you will be in thinking up ways to have a good time. This is part of your contribution to the partnership. Of course what you arrange will depend on where you live, what is available to you, and your parents co-operation.

You may plan quiet home dates when your boy friend helps you with that math assignment you couldn't get, and you treat him to the brownies you made that afternoon. You might invite another couple to share the fun of preparing a special dish for dinner.

Double dates? Marge and Ted and Wendy and Bob double date a lot. Ted has a car which he generously shares with Bob and his date. They have a livelier time when they double date than when one couple goes alone, and they find it easier to keep the gay conversation going.

Not all double dating turns out so well. When couples have different tastes and standards, different ideas about what is fun, about drinking, necking, places to go and time to get home, a double date can prove to be an uncomfortable affair. It works best with friends you know and like, and when you have agreed beforehand where you will go and what time you will get home.

You don't have to have a pine-paneled game room in order to get the crowd together. If you live in a house with a garage, attic or basement, make the most of it. Use your ingenuity in fixing it up and planning informal good times.

Picnics and cook-outs can be memorable occasions when everybody has a hand in the work and the fun.

If you live in an apartment, there are many things you can plan for a home date. Fran and Deb, a fairly sophisticated pair of college freshmen, told us, "You can play cards, chess, or other games. You can put together a jigsaw puzzle. You can play your records or watch television. Boys and girls enjoy these opportunities to chat and get to know one another. Of course, you can have parties and dance in apartments too, if you are careful not to overdo it and disturb your neighbors."

Let's go back for a moment to that first date for a special occasion. Your boy friend had arranged to call for you at a certain time. You remember that boys who are new at this sort of thing too are often uncertain and shy, so you are careful to be dressed and on hand to introduce him to your parents. "Mother," you say, "this is Bill," and you add, "you remember, his mother was my fifth grade teacher." You have thought of this bit about Bill earlier so that he and your mother will have something to talk about.

You give your parents a few minutes to talk to Bill, and then you say something about getting started, and pick up your coat, if you are going to wear one. You accept Bill's help graciously if he offers it, or put on the coat without fuss, if he doesn't. You say good night to your parents, telling them where you are going and what time they may expect you home. You have probably talked all this over with them earlier, but this makes it unnecessary for them to go into any heavy parent act, and lets Bill know what curfew hour he will have to keep.

When that curfew hour arrives and Bill has you safely on your doorstep, must you kiss him good night? Do you invite him in?

If your lighted house tells you that your parents are still

up, there's no reason why you shouldn't ask him in if you wish to. Your mother may have suggested you ask him to try her famous chocolate cake instead of stopping at the local Sweet Shoppe. If there's a low light burning for you, it's your cue to say, "I've had such a good time, Bill. You certainly know how to make a date fun." Add good night and slip unhesitatingly inside your door as if there were nothing new or difficult in this for you, who have had boys bringing you home from dates without number.

What about that good-night kiss? Boys on first dates wonder whether girls expect it. Girls say some boys try them out to see what they will do. Many girls dislike the promiscuous kissing of every boy, any boy, on a first date. They reserve the good-night kiss until they have been out with a boy several times and know and like him well enough to want to kiss him.

Expressions of affection are warm and natural with people you like. Don't be a prude and make a mountain out of a friendly kiss. When you have had a pleasant evening with a boy you like, you may want to kiss him good night. You may want to kiss him at other times too—if he brings you an especially thoughtful gift or corsage of your favorite flower, on his birthday, or when he has gained some honor or won some sports event.

What about demonstrations of affection that go beyond a good-night kiss? In your grandmother's day the word was spoon, and it rhymed with croon, moon and June. Nowadays we talk of necking and petting instead of spooning. Because the rules and conventions are not so hard and fast as they were in the spooning days, girls are often confused. They want to know what we mean by these words; if there is a difference between them; what is permissible; if a girl must pet to be popular.

Necking. Usually necking means the kind of harmless

expressions of affection that do not involve sex, as for instance when a boy puts his arm around a girl, or she leans her head on his shoulder and they exchange a brief kiss. This is a normal and natural way to express the feeling they have for each other. They are learning to show affection for the opposite sex without self-consciousness or embarrassment; they are finding out how to be warm and outgoing in their relationships with others.

If such gestures of affection are prolonged or repeated too often, they lose their charm and run into the danger of becoming more and more passionate until the young couple, with or without any such intent, are petting.

Petting. Petting means prolonged and passionate kissing, and caressing parts of the body that stimulate sex urges. This kind of love-making should come only after marriage. But statistics tell a sad tale of a rising number of unmarried mothers of high school age. When you think about nature's intention in designing the sexual system, you can easily understand that two people far from ready for marriage, have no business indulging in petting. Many strict social regulations have been relaxed in the years in which spooning became petting—but don't let anyone fool you, the position of the unmarried mother is only slightly less difficult. Sex, properly controlled, is a fine and wonderful thing, but it is a force too powerful for inexperienced young people to play with.

Yet girls ask if they must pet to be popular. Quite the contrary, really, if you mean the kind of popularity that makes a girl and her parents proud. Who wants a date with a different boy every night in the week, if the boys are only interested in finding out whether what they heard about you is true? Or if their only concern is easily obtained sexual excitement? Boys talk, and such dubious popularity could be extremely embarrassing. Guilty feelings can have the power later to spoil what should be happy experiences.

Girls may tell you that if you don't pet you are a prude and the boys won't date you. Boys may try to make you believe the same thing. Some boys think a casual date entitles them to make advances. Others try a girl out to see how far they can go, and they have little respect for the girl they label "willing." Still others say girls think they are slow if they don't "make passes." And there are some who assure you that love such as you two share is rare and enduring, if you do not kill it by your coldness. No matter what the excuse or the argument, make up your mind that petting is not for you.

The wise girl plans her dates so that she goes somewhere or does something. She never agrees to an evening spent in a parked car beside a moonlit lake. If she likes a boy a lot, she limits her expressions of affection to the few minutes when she says good night at her door. For her, kisses are not the main event on a date, but the climax of an evening of fun. She manages these things so as to avoid situations in which opportunities for petting may arise. If in spite of her best maneuvers, the question comes up, she makes it immediately clear that this sort of thing does not appeal to her. It is the girl who dictates in such matters and who must never hesitate to assume the responsibility, for she may pay in damaged reputation if she permits things to get out of hand.

Gifts. "My boy friend has a birthday next month, and I don't know whether I should give him a present," writes a worried reader. It is natural to express fondness for friends, girls and boys, by presents at Christmas or on birthdays. An expensive gift is poor taste and likely to embarrass him. But something you have made yourself— socks, mittens, hand-rolled monogrammed handkerchief—

or some small item that shows you take an interest in him and are aware of his special tastes—a trout fly, golf gloves—will tell him that you appreciate his friendship.

Boys often "say it with flowers" at Christmas, on birthdays, for the special dance or game, when a girl is ill, or in a play, or on any other occasion when a gesture of appreciation is in order. Whether it is an expensive hothouse corsage or a posy from the garden, whether or not it is your favorite flower, whether or not it clashes with your dress, take care not to hurt the boy's feelings. Show him you value the thoughtfulness that prompted the gift.

What do you do if a boy gives you an expensive present which you would rather not accept and probably won't be allowed to keep? You make your appreciation of his thoughtfulness and generosity very clear and tell him simply that you are sorry but your parents would not want you to accept so costly a gift.

People who are fond of one another express their feelings in words too. When a boy pays you a sincere compliment, do you shrug it off, belittling his good opinion and changing the subject? You're embarrassed, and your confusion embarrasses him. Try smiling straight at the boy and saying simply, "Thank you, Bob, I am glad you think so." He will feel pleased with himself and happy at having pleased you. Like everything else connected with dating and your new grown-up social life, it will grow easier as you practice.

Going Dutch. "Special occasions such as proms are frightfully expensive," girls say. "Boys have to pay for the tickets, hire tuxedos, buy flowers, and take us somewhere afterward to eat. What about going Dutch? Can girls share expenses?" Just as boys cherish their masculine prerogative of making the dates and the telephone calls, they feel that they lose face unless they assume the expenses of a date. If you are sincere in your feeling that the cost of the big prom—easily fifty dollars or more in metropolitan districts—is too much for a teen-age boy, why not do something about it? Especially if you are a popular girl, you can be a leader in bringing the matter up in class meeting, taking it up with the faculty and P.T.A. In some communities girls have ruled out formal dress for their escorts, and corsages for themselves. Parents have worked together to plan after-the-dance suppers or breakfasts that contribute to everyone's peace of mind by dispensing with the cost of restaurants and night clubs, the hazard of night driving to more or less distant night spots, and wild, unchaperoned parties.

Of course you embarrass a boy if you attempt to buy your ticket to the movies or pay your share of a restaurant check. If he has taken you out frequently and you want to reciprocate, you will have to do it tactfully by entertaining him at your house, inviting him to your parties. You can arrange a picnic for which you take the lunch. You might secure in advance tickets for a play or game for a night on which you have a date with him, and give them to him with a careful word of explanation that you have tickets and are glad you have a date with him for that night so that you can use them together.

Going steady. Now you have had several dates with Bill, and here he is offering you his class ring and asking you to go steady? What's the answer? Again, there is no easy yes or no. What you mean by going steady may be more or less serious according to local custom. Often a girl wears a boy's class ring or his identification bracelet, and so announces to her friends and classmates that she is dating one boy exclusively. Other boys will no longer feel free to ask her for dates. Even without a visible token, going steady usually means that a girl agrees to confine her dates to one boy until they end the arrangement by mutual consent.

Let's consider what some girls feel are the advantages of going steady. If you cling to old friends and find getting acquainted difficult, you may be happiest with one boy with whom you can share experiences and confidences. You prefer inexpensive evenings at the movies or playing canasta at home with your steady date, rather than some more exciting date with a boy you hardly know. Of course you have the security of an escort for all the games and dances. You share interests and take up new ones together. You feel that you are gaining experience in loyalty, consideration, learning to understand masculine actions and reactions, putting another's interest above your own and getting along together that will stand you in good stead later when you marry.

But going steady means, too, that you play fair and live up to your agreement not to date other boys for any reason. So if your steady is away or not available for some social occasion, you stay at home. It means that you are willing to take a chance on the loneliness that can come to you if for any reason your twosome breaks up.

On the contrary, if you enjoy change, like excitement, think quiet evenings at home are too boring, crave to be doing something different all the time and get a kick out of the compliments, kidding and attentions of boys (plural), going steady is not your dish.

Besides getting an education, one of the important things you should be accomplishing during your teens is getting to know various persons of the opposite sex. If you start going steady in the early dating years, you cut yourself off from opportunities to meet and know different boys. How can you find out what boys are like, and what kind of boy will be most compatible, if you tie yourself down to the first boy you date?

Unfortunately, in some high schools the custom of going

steady is so widely and firmly established a girl must go along with it or be left out of the social life. In such a case, you may find yourself going steady not because the boy is especially attractive to you, but merely to make sure you have a date and won't miss out on the dances and other events. In some schools, you may find that you are going steady if you accept three or four dates in a row with the same boy. The idea may not have occurred to either of you, but your friends have it all neatly arranged for you, and other boys will not date you.

Girls have defeated this system by talking it over with their girl and boy friends and letting it be known that they do not intend to go along with the idea. You might get the debating team to make it the subject of one of their sessions, or have a panel discussion in one of your social studies classes. Get the faculty and the P.T.A. interested in helping to abolish the practice. You will have to hold your end up carefully by avoiding too many successive dates with the same boy.

It may not always be easy and you may miss an event or two, but you might be glad to settle for this, when you weigh it against being tagged as Jim's girl, when Jim is really not at all your cup of tea.

All the girls in Ruth's crowd wore the class rings of their steadies. When Dave offered her his, she couldn't resist accepting it in order to be like the others and have a ring to wear. In January, he went south for a month with his parents. Ruth sat at home, furious with herself because now it was all too plain that she did not care enough for Dave to make him the only boy in her life. She was good sport enough not to tell him this in a letter, but when he came home she gave him back his ring so tactfully that they are still good friends and see each other occasionally, though they both date others. "Maybe we'll find that we are really suited to each other as time passes," Ruth says, "but we are giving ourselves a chance to grow up first and develop into the kind of persons we want to be. Next time, if there is a next time, we'll be a whole lot surer of our feelings for each other before we make any exclusive pledges."

Ruth had learned something many couples find out when they go away to college. As their minds and personalities develop, they often outgrow their high school steadies.

The girl who dates one boy exclusively must handle the situation carefully to avoid becoming more deeply involved than she wishes to be. Too much time spent alone with the boy may lead to more and more love-making until control slips. There is the risk of the too early marriage of two persons not mature enough to face up to their responsibilities or to choose the partners who will satisfy their adult needs.

Bea had gone steady with Andy for several months. Gradually she realized that he was beginning to bore her. She did not enjoy the same things as Andy, and she was tired of pretending. What now, she asked herself, for Andy was a nice boy and she was fond of him. How do you break off the going steady relationship? It takes courage and tact. Talk it over as considerately as you can, telling the boy that you are beginning to feel that going steady is not for you. Make every effort to avoid hurting his feelings and damaging his pride. After you have settled the question between yourselves, let your friends know about it so they will not continue to pair you together.

It sometimes takes a little time to get back again into circulation. Your friends can help with invitations and double dates. Start again as you did when you were beginning to date by going places where you don't need an escort. Take up new interests and do some of the things you had to drop while your steady date was taking up all your time.

Unlike Bea, Sally really cared for her steady date, Jeff, and she was heartbroken when he became infatuated with a blond senior. But Sally had spunk. She determinedly cut short her grieving for her lost love and took steps to get over him. She got rid of everything that reminded her of him—snapshots, records, letters, gifts. She had always been interested in photography, so she joined the Camera Club. Here she met a whole new group of friends who welcomed her as a fellow shutter-bug on their field trips. Whenever Sally found herself lapsing back into thoughts of Jeff, she grabbed her camera and went picture hunting.

First dates, corsages, proms, first kisses—it's all thrilling and exciting. It's like a gay game. That's fine, as long as both boy and girl understand it's a game. Marge loved only herself. To her it was a lark to keep as many boys as she could dancing attendance on her. Because she was incapable of deep feeling herself, she could not imagine that Fred was really serious about her. For the last two years of high school she allowed him to think she cared as much for him as he did for her, while she knew all the time that he really meant nothing to her. When she threw him over at the last minute to go to the senior prom with another, Fred was so deeply hurt it took him a long, long time to get over it.

Warm-hearted, womanly girls are concerned about the boys they date. They are honest with them and do not treat lightly the regard in which the boys hold them. Romance is the sweet and the spice of your teen years. But the girl who can make real friends of the boys she dates often keeps their affection as she does that of her girl friends all her life.

And now you have been dating long enough to feel

sure of yourself. You remember your long-ago dream and you smile. Hasn't it almost come true? You *are* poised and confident. Sometimes you even think you are almost pretty. There are boys around you and it's wonderful, and you wouldn't change places with anyone in the world.

CHAPTER EIGHT

BE POISED

How can I learn social poise—and overcome my awkwardness?

What plans do you need to make if you are giving a party?

What duties have I as a hostess? Have I any as a guest?

How do I introduce guests to one another; to my parents?

Can you entertain friends if your home is small and shabby?

How can I learn good table manners?

Four girls were sitting on the library steps when the new student, a boy from far across the country, came out of the big double doors. Jill called out a friendly greeting. "I'm glad you can come to my party next Tuesday, Bob," she said, and added, "I'm looking forward to introducing you to my friends."

Ruth hardly heard the boy's answer, she was so consumed with jealousy of Jill's poise. Jill always knew just what to do or say. She was never awkward or tongue-tied as Ruth so often was. Jill, Ruth thought enviously, would never have the jitters over giving a party—nor cold chills about the right thing to do when she was a guest. Ruth was more than ever convinced that some people are born with social know-how.

Don't you believe it. Not even a royal baby comes into this world with any instinctive knowledge of what is socially correct. Manners are not only a matter of geography (what is good form in Damascus may be inexcusable in Daytona) but also of training and practice. Jill has probably been learning from her babyhood through precept, example and practice, how to be at ease in any social situation. You—or Ruth or the girl next door—can acquire Jill's poise, if you care enough to find out what is expected of you socially and practice, practice, practice until it *is* instinctive.

For the techniques of social skill—what we sometimes call etiquette—like those of art and music are partly a matter of learning the rules and putting them into practice. But no matter how good the technique, the painting or the song will lack greatness without something that springs from the heart. So it is with manners.

Jill was relaxed and at ease because she was sincerely interested in the lonely boy and wanted to make him happy. That was why she had invited him to one of her parties. Thoughtfulness of others, which means forgetfulness of self, will give you the sort of social ease that no mere adherence to formal rules of etiquette can ever equal.

When you think of social skills, it's natural that you should think of parties, for they loom large on any teenager's expanding horizon. We spoke of parties earlier as one of the ways for girls to get boys started dating. Though boys demand the initiative in asking for dates they are often too hesitant about their own social adequacy in their early teens to take it.

Jill had the good fortune to have a mother who realized this, anticipated Jill's need to establish friendly contacts with boys, and arranged her first boy-and-girl parties. If you are not so lucky, you will have to make the effort yourself. When you have made friends with a group of girls, join them for a coke after school, ask them to lunch on Saturday. You'll soon find that you are accepted as one of the crowd or that you have formed your own crowd. Don't be afraid to branch out and invite the boys to join you. It is fine to be loyal to your girl friends, but you do not need to spend all your time with them. Remember one of the important things you should be learning during your teen years is how to get along socially with the opposite sex.

Often two or three girls join together to have a party. They find this an excellent way to break into society composed of two sexes. The boys they help in this way to overcome their awkward feeling of social inexperience are emboldened later to ask the girls for dates. The experience the girls gain will be valuable to them when they become mistresses of their own homes someday. Hospitality is a warm and gracious thing and they will be grateful when it comes easily and naturally to them.

But right now, like Ruth, you may be worried about whether or not you are competent to undertake a party. Will you know what to do? Are you afraid your parents will disgrace you by some act contrary to teen-age standards of approval? Will your home and what you have to offer be acceptable?

Whether you fulfill your duties and responsibilities as hostess alone or share them with friends, you will be more at ease if you plan carefully in advance of the party date. Invite your friends far enough ahead—about ten days or two weeks—so that they will be free to accept. Formal invitations are likely to make your friends feel stiff and uncomfortable and to lead them to expect elaborate refreshments and entertainment. You will be nervous about living up to all this, and your guests will be worried about their own social competence instead of anticipating a good time. Informal invitations over the telephone, or gay and amusing notes in line with the theme of the party, if it has one, give promise of more fun. Be sure to include date, time, and place.

If you consider your guest list carefully and invite people who have similar tastes and interests, much of the success of your party will be assured. Even an experienced hostess can fail if her guests don't mix or are unfriendly. It's obviously not a good idea to include the boy with whom Jean has just broken off, if you are asking Jean and her new boy friend.

Decide in advance what, if anything, you plan to have in the way of decorations. Everyone is likely to have more fun if you keep things simple. Of course you want your house to look its best, but don't carry it to such extremes that you wear yourself out cleaning and fussing and are too tired to enjoy your guests. You invite your friends to have a pleasant time, not to show off your home or your possessions. They will be a good deal more interested in having fun than in the luxury or austerity of your facilities for entertaining. The most successful hostess shares whatever she has joyously, without apology no matter how meager, and by her own pleasure in their company makes her guests glad they came.

Keep your menu simple. You and your guests will be more comfortable if you have things much as they generally are in your home. You are likely to run into embarrassing predicaments and to show strain that will make both you and your guests uneasy, if you attempt unusual and elaborate food, decorations or activities.

Make a list of the food and other things you need and

do your shopping the day before the party. Aim for simple refreshments that you can either prepare in advance or invite your guests to share in preparing. You'll be surprised at how quickly this sort of participation makes a shy guest feel at ease.

Of course you will give thought in advance to what you plan to do in the way of entertainment. A good idea is to alternate dancing or lively activities with quiet games. You will find books of games on the shelves of your local library. Look up square dances, Paul Jones mixers, so that you have suggestions to offer if the boys huddle in a group by themselves, or an older couple seem inclined to cuddle together in a corner. Your plans should be flexible. You don't want to put your guests through routines like a top sergeant. Merely have things in mind and on hand to use as need arises.

It is your responsibility to see that the fun does not get out of hand or endanger your parents' home or its furnishings. If the roughhousing of a boy not yet mature enough for teen-age parties imperils a lamp or a vase, don't encourage him. Switch to another game that will interest all the guests and cause them to ignore him. If he persists, you will have to ask him politely to stop and tell him that you are sorry but if he does not behave you will not be permitted to have him in your house again.

It's your duty to make sure that everyone joins in the fun and has a good time. You may have to make a special effort to get a shy boy or girl into the group. You don't need to work so hard at this that you don't have any fun yourself. If you fuss over your guests until they are burdened by your attentions, they are uncomfortable.

You will want your parents on hand to greet your guests. They need not suffer the noise of your youthful high spirits and nonsense all evening, but they should be nearby in case of a need. Perhaps your mother will help you with the refreshments. Your neighbors and the parents of your friends will be glad to know that there are adults at home when you entertain.

As your guests arrive you introduce them to each other and to your parents. You remember that you present the boys to the girls, and boys and girls first to your mother and then to your father. If you think of some small identifying phrase so much the better. "Mary," you say, "this is Bill. He suffers with me over accents in French II." Or, "Dad, this is Mary. She made that poster for Sports Night you admired so much." This grows easier the more you practice.

It is sometimes awkward when a party is large to introduce a late guest to everyone. Rather than pilot her around a circle, reeling off names she won't remember, introduce her to the group nearest you and let your friends carry on from there. Of course, your guest speaks to fellow guests whether or not she has been formally introduced. When a boy who has not been presented to her speaks to her, she says, "I am Mary Brown." He will respond with his name. She follows this procedure also in talking to a strange girl or to any adults who may be present.

The accepted reply to an introduction is that question to which no one ever expects an answer, "How do you do?" You may repeat the name of the person who has just been introduced if you wish. Men shake hands. Women may or may not, as they please. Of course if a hand is extended, it would be ungracious to ignore it, so you shake hands.

The size of a house and the luxuriousness of its appointments are no measure of the success of hospitality. You know your own facilities for entertaining. If you have an outdoor grill or a fireplace, suppers at which everyone works at preparing the food are fun, and later you and your guests may sing or tell ghost stories around the fire. If you have a large living room, a basement or game room, share them with your friends. If your family is large and your home small, so that you have no place at all to entertain, you might plan a picnic at a beach, a park or a lakeside. Use your imagination, your inventiveness, to share a little gracious gaiety and fun with your friends and to reciprocate the hospitality they have offered you.

You may be missing out on the social experience you should be acquiring and the fun you should be having during your teens because you feel there is a prejudice against your religious or racial group or you think your family's income or social standing is less privileged than that of other girls. Often there is no real basis for such feelings, but sometimes oversensitive teen-agers worry because their homes seem shabby, their parents do not belong to clubs, and their family standard of living seems less luxurious than that of others. They behave in a stiff, unnatural, unfriendly manner which prevents others from getting to know them.

If there is truth in your feeling of rejection, don't be discouraged. Don't become embittered, rather take from your experience a wider understanding and thoughtfulness of others. Make the most of your abilities and sooner or later you will find friends who accept you, not for your background, but for what you are.

Ruth was sometimes uncertain about what to do as a guest. *Do you have any special duties and responsibilities when you are a guest?* Indeed you do, if you want to be a popular one who is asked again and again. Anticipate the party in a positive manner with the thought firmly in mind that you are going to have a good time. Never let the idea that you are going to be a wallflower enter your mind.

Don't giggle or gush, but be enthusiastic and ready to have fun at every opportunity. A blasé pseudosophisticated guest who is pleased with nothing can ruin the best party. Be relaxed, comfortable, at home, joining in whatever is going on without tension or embarrassment. Greet your hostess and her parents when they arrive. Be polite and interested in any other members of the family who are present, but do not overwhelm the hostess' father, who jokes with you, or her handsome older brother, with too much attention.

If refreshments are served at table, remain standing by your chair until your hostess is seated. Unfold your napkin about half when your hostess does and place it across your knees. When the hostess rises from the table, place it as it is, half-folded, on the table. No teen-ager needs to be warned not to talk with her mouth full, to wipe her mouth before drinking from her glass, or to sip her soup silently.

You usually wait until everyone is served before beginning to eat, but if it is a large party and the food is hot, you may begin when those around you have been served. It is polite to take a little of anything offered you, whether or not you like it. If you cannot eat it, leave it on your plate without comment. While eating, place your knife across the upper right edge of the plate and your fork in the center of the plate. When passing your plate or at the end of a meal, place the knife and fork together near the center of the plate. If oyster cocktails are the first course, pick up each oyster with your oyster fork, dip it in the sauce at the center, and swallow the oyster whole. Leave any remaining sauce. If you are served soup in a cup with handles, you may drink it if you wish. Usually you use the soup spoon to dip the soup away from you, and then sip it from the side of the spoon. You eat the accompanying crackers separately, but if croutons are served, place some on your butter plate and drop two or three at a time in your soup.

Vegetables served in a side dish should be eaten from the dish with a fork if possible. When the sauce is very liquid, use a spoon and place it on your dinner plate when you have finished. Break a baked potato open with your fingers and mix butter, pepper and salt into a third of it at a time, with your fork. When eating meat cut up a few pieces and transfer your fork to your right hand to eat them, then back to the left hand to cut up some more meat. In Europe it is the custom to cut your meat and eat it with the fork in the left hand. Salad should be eaten with the fork alone, but if you are served head lettuce, you may cut it with your knife. The large lettuce leaf under mixed salad may be eaten. Help yourself to bread, rolls, sandwiches with your fingers, never with a fork. Break off small pieces of bread or rolls and butter them as you eat them. Large sandwiches should be broken or, if this can not be done neatly, cut with your knife and fork.

If refreshments are served buffet style, help yourself to plate, napkin, the required silver, and serve yourself to the dishes of your choice from the serving plates on the table.

Anyone may have the misfortune to spill something at table. If it happens to you, say you are sorry, wipe it up if necessary, and forget it. It will not help to dwell on it aloud to your hostess, or to agonize over it in your own mind. If you are unlucky enough to break something, apologize and if possible replace it. If replacement is impossible, don't fail to express to the parents of your hostess your regret and your desire to make what amends you can.

If you must leave early, don't hesitate to do so. You needn't say, "Dad insists I must be home by eleven." Instead you might say something to the effect that you hate to tear yourself away from such a gay party, but you have an early engagement tomorrow and you have to leave. Do so quietly without disturbing the other guests. Don't dawdle for ten or fifteen minutes, keeping your hostess away from the others. Thank her and her parents sincerely for their hospitality and leave promptly.

Make the most of your teen years in learning how to act with poise on social occasions. The first years are the most difficult. Each added experience puts you more at ease, so seek them out, never shun them. As you keep learning, it becomes easier. All your life the skills of friendly courtesy will make you welcome anywhere.

CHAPTER NINE

JOB WANTED!

*How can I find a part-time job—and decide if it's
the best one for me?*
*Is it better to work after school on week days—or
on Saturdays?*
What sort of summer jobs are open to girls?
*If I earn money baby-sitting, what important things
should I know?*
Does the law say anything about teen-age workers?

"A teen-ager's perpetual problem is money!" Kathy declares.
"Very few of us girls have a big enough allowance to stretch
around everything—fun with the gang, clothes for school
and dates and dances. If you want to do things like everybody else, the answer is, earn some money of your own.
Just ask any girl."

We have. The Girl Scout study revealed that 70 per cent
of all the girls interviewed across the United States earn
some part of the money they spend. Four out of five high
school girls have jobs for which they are paid. And a great
many others are clamoring to know what they can do—
where, and when and how they can earn money.

"Is it just for the sake of making two ends meet and
keeping in the swim that girls work?" we asked Kathy.
"What about the girl whose parents can afford to give her

107

everything she needs? Do you think she would want a job?"

She came back at us quickly. "Yes, I think she might. Take my best friend, Hilda. Her dad would buy her anything she asked for. He says she makes him look like a tightwad by going around the neighborhood baby-sitting. Her mother insists it's just a fad she'll get over. But it isn't."

"What is it, then?"

"Well, Hilda says she doesn't want to run to her parents for everything. If she does they'll always treat her like a child. Parents never want you to grow up. But if they see you earning money of your own they respect you more, and they let you have more say about everything."

It's true: earned money buys things—it also creates a sense of maturity and independence. There's nothing perhaps quite like it for giving you a toe hold on the adult world, where people are often rated by their earning power. A job can teach you to stand on your own feet, accept responsibility, get along with others. It may show bigger returns than *just* the dollars and cents you stow away in the pocket of your jeans.

Of course, right now, your biggest job is in your school books—and we know you are smart enough not to neglect that, for it's one job that will pay off later on. But many people agree that a little practical work experience, and even some reasonably strenuous physical effort, will help make the "book learning" come to life. Learning to *think* is important—but so is learning to *do!*

So back to the big question. *What are the ways of earning money in the teen years?*

Ingenious teen-agers have found that there are many— whether it be after-school jobs, Saturday jobs, or jobs in the summer after school has closed. But before you start looking around or deciding on anything, it might be well to take a fast inventory of yourself, and also to weigh some of the factors involved.

A good objective appraisal of *yourself* ought to include the answers to such questions as: How much health and physical endurance do I have—can I manage a job and schoolwork, too, plus a reasonable amount of social life? What sort of person am I—the quiet sort, who likes to work alone; the gay, sociable kind who is happiest doing things with other people? Do I like little children, and have I had experience caring for little brothers and sisters? Have I tastes or hobbies that could be put to good account in earning money—painting, writing, dancing, cooking, sewing, gardening, raising pets, photography, or something else? Have I had secretarial courses at school—am I pretty good at typing, stenography, filing, and other office routines?

Baby-sitting. A hard look at yourself may give you ideas for earning money that you had not thought about before. Terry likes baby-sitting because she adores little children— even those at her own house who sometimes raise a racket when she tries to get her studying done. The Carmichaels' baby is only two. Once Terry gets her bathed and to bed, she has a quiet place to study until the parents return home—and she's paid besides! "It's a swell deal!" Terry says. The Carmichaels agree with her. They like the way she handles their little daughter, and her sense of responsibility.

Terry did miss a date last week that she very much wanted to accept. Ken stopped her between classes at school to say his cousin Peter was in town for just twenty-four hours. They'd like to double date Terry and her girl friend that evening. Could she make it? She shook her head sadly. She'd already agreed to be at the Carmichaels by seven, and she knew they had tickets for the theater.

For a moment she thought of asking Ken and his friends to drop by there later—but that was definitely against the rules. She had to tell Ken he'd have to date another girl.

Before we leave the baby-sitting subject, there are some very important things that need to be said. If you do go in for earning money this way, make sure that you are well prepared. If your school, or the local Safety Council, or Red Cross chapter, or Girl Scout Council, has arranged for a course in baby-sitting, take it if you possibly can. You may be reliable and conscientious, yet by no means ready for some of the situations that can arise.

A number of organizations, including the United States Children's Bureau, the National Safety Council, and the Girl Scouts of the U.S.A., have devised rules for the safety both of the sitter herself and of the children for whom she is caring. Let's have a look at these and pick out some of the most important ones.

DO: Keep beside the telephone on your sitter's job the numbers where the parents, family doctor, police and fire department can be reached in an emergency. Place a rubber mat or turkish towel in the tub when bathing a child. Watch that he does not trip on the stairs or explore the bathroom medicine closet. Peep in to see that he is covered when asleep, but not smothering himself with the bedclothes. Baby-sit only for families known to you or your friends, or thoroughly investigated. Write down the names of any callers or deliveries expected, and open the door only to these. Arrive on time, ask if you may use the TV or radio, arrange to be accompanied home if you do not live close by. Be affectionate and cheerful—but firm with your charge.

DON'T: Agree to care for a sick child or administer medicine. Become so absorbed in book or TV that you forget to check on your small charge frequently. Admit strangers to the house, entertain the boy friend, or even have a girl friend in without special permission. Raid the refrigerator (you can bring along a sandwich). Try to manage a small child by scolding, punishment or threats—the negative approach does not work!

Before you decide on any job, you should weigh very carefully the obligations it will place on you, the responsibility those who hire you and pay you have a right to expect. Perhaps this appraisal will convince you the money earned isn't worth the sacrifice. Then that is the job you should pass up. Look around for something else, more appealing to you, and which you can carry out with full sincerity.

A week-end job. An older girl sometimes prefers a Saturday job to one like baby-sitting that can interfere with a date. Beth was very good at secretarial work. She found a local shopkeeper who had need of a secretary—but not full time. He hired her to work for him Saturdays from nine to one, keeping his simple account books in order, making out bills, typing a few letters and orders to wholesalers. "For me, it's the ideal job," Beth says. "And it's giving me practice, plus a reference, when I look for a full-time job later on."

Mary would not like Beth's job at all. She's an outdoor girl, and the bunch she goes with have the same tastes. Often they go on an all-day Saturday hike, or a week-end camping trip, summer or winter—and she would be left behind. But Mary's outdoor interests led her to something else in the money-making line—photography. For several years, her camping equipment has always included a camera. Last year at Christmas her dad gave her a very good one, and she has learned to develop her own pictures at home. She has a beautiful collection of photos—including birds and small animals as well as scenic views.

Mary tried to think how she could turn her skill in photography to profit—and she came up with a good idea. On pleasant afternoons, she goes out looking for shots she will probably be able to sell. A small child playing on a doorstep; a new home that has just been completed; two brothers romping with their dog in the snow; a garden in bloom; a house front beautifully decorated for Christmas. When she goes back later with her prints—yes, she built an enlarger with her dad's help—she more often than not finds delighted customers, who encourage her to "call again."

Donna and Marge are two sixteen-year-olds with a great common interest: dancing. They have had some instruction in ballet and tap—but they love almost anything that will keep your feet moving to music, from square dancing to cha cha. One day Donna said, "You know, Marg, we could make money with this!"

Marg was doubtful. "Dad would never let me dance in a night club, nor anything like that."

"Of course not! But wouldn't he let you have a dancing class for eight-year-olds? I'll bet lots of parents would be happy to have their kids learn—and the youngsters would have a wonderful time! We could charge a small fee, and hold the class in my recreation room."

The junior dance groups Donna and Marg started are so popular they have to turn boys and girls away. They meet each Wednesday afternoon and Saturday morning. Now the girls have been asked to organize a dance group at the junior high level. They'll teach square dances, and the principal says they can use a room in the school.

Earning money can be fun, if you fit it to your personal talents. Edith is very artistic, is interested in fashion design, has done some rather striking posters for the dramatic club at school, and has even been commissioned a few times to do a poster for the local Garden or Rotary Club.

Someday she hopes to have a career in commercial art, but that will take further study after high school. In the meantime, she kept turning over in her mind how she could earn a little cash pretty regularly at something in line with her big interest.

Good ideas, like charity, often begin at home. Edith's real break came one day when she noticed how dull and uninteresting the window of her dad's hardware store looked. It was much the same as she had always known it for years, with a clutter of unrelated and unbeautiful items —plumbing supplies, farm implements, fishing tackle, a washing machine, buckets and basins and gadgets of every kind. "What it needs is more drama," she said to herself. And then she went to her dad. "Dad, how about letting me try some window dressing? Your window isn't good bait. I know lots of people come here for things they need—but a lot of them wait to do their shopping when they go to the city, even though they carry home the same things they could get here in our town."

Edith's dad was not convinced, but he humored her and let her try. She did a stuffed figure of a farmer's wife— life-size and comical, with yellow floss for hair, her cheeks a rosy red, her waist swathed in a big gingham apron. And then she placed her funny rag-doll woman in front of a nice new washing machine in the center of the window, with all the gadgets removed. Result: people came to look and laugh and buy things. Her window dressing worked wonders for Dad, and other shopkeepers in town asked her to do some for them. Edith gets a nice fee, and has a lot of fun with her original ideas. She's also sold the idea that window dressings should be changed often enough to keep the customers dropping past to have a look. That keeps her in business.

"Don't overdo it though!" Nellie warns. "Whatever way

you choose to earn money, don't overdo your own strength. I love to bake cakes and pies, and I went around taking week-end orders. Pretty soon I had so many customers I was exhausted with the Saturday baking and delivery— and Mother was so upset over the mess in her kitchen she said it had to stop. I found it wasn't fun after all, but a lot of hard work. Now I have a regular Saturday job as cashier in a neighborhood store, and I like it a lot better. It's more gay and sociable, meeting the people who keep coming in."

Nellie's sister profited by this mistake. She likes cooking and baking, too, but she went at it another way. She worked up a list of clients who call on her to help when they are giving a party, or having special guests for dinner —or when they just want to relax and let somebody else prepare a good meal. Every week she has a few requests by phone, and takes on as many as she feels she can handle.

Help in getting a job. Sometimes the girl in a big city feels that the small-towner has more opportunities for money-making than she. She is apt to fall back on baby-sitting as her only resource. Let her give a good look around her. It is true that city life can sometimes appear impersonal and bewildering—but it holds many opportunities for the teen-ager to find a part-time job.

City high schools often do a great deal to help their students earn money through part-time jobs that are suited to their capabilities. Many schools have a counselor who will discuss with you your aptitudes and the jobs available. She may be better able to size up your personality and your physical strength than you are, and to make suggestions that will put you on the right track. If there is such a counselor in your school, talk to her frankly—but of course make up your own mind.

Many large high schools have a part-time employment bureau to help young people find work. In others, the students themselves have organized a part-time employment committee with a faculty adviser. Such a bureau or student committee makes contacts with local employers and social agencies, and receives calls from those who have suitable openings. If your school has no such plan in operation, talk with your teacher or counselor and perhaps you can help get something of this nature started.

During World War II, when workers were sorely needed, many high schools instituted what was known as the four-four plan, by which students of senior high school age who met health and aptitude qualifications, were given scholastic credit for work they did on the outside. Under proper supervision, groups of teen-agers worked four hours a day in a local industry or store, or in gathering the harvest in rural areas, thus freeing older men and women for work in the war plants or military services. This co-operative plan of work and study proved successful in actually stimulating the interest of young people in their schoolwork, as well as helping them to discover their vocational interests. And so, today, the co-operative plan is finding favor in a number of localities. Perhaps it is in yours.

Working at different jobs is certainly the best way to explore the vocational field. If you have dreamed of a career—or just a future job that will fill the gap between school and marriage, it is not a bad idea to have a go at it now in a small way, and see how you really like it. Girls who take part-time clerking jobs in a large department store often discover there is a real future in becoming a sales person and, with experience, a full-fledged buyer in charge of a particular line of merchandise. The home economics student who works as a waitress or hostess in a restaurant, may decide to prepare for a career as a dietitian. The nurse's aide will have a chance to test the true degree of her interest in nursing—and the same holds good for the library aide, the playground assistant, the assistant in social work.

Maybe after you have thought it over, you've decided that, while you need to earn money—say, to meet the expenses you see looming in your senior high school year, or to finance your clothes bill and other expenses for college—you would rather wait and take a full-time summer job, and thus leave yourself free for winter social activities.

Depending on the person you are, the difficulties you may be having with your schoolwork, your health, the home situation, and a number of other things only you can judge, that may be a wise decision. Talk it over with your parents; their advice can be useful in this.

Summer jobs. In summer, there are many supervised groups of senior girls, as well as boys, who do work on farms and love it. If you cannot find out about such possibilities through your school, ask the local branch of the United States Employment Service, or write to the Women's Bureau, Department of Labor, Washington, D.C., for information. You could ask them, too, for a list of suggested summer jobs for girls.

Eleanor, at seventeen, with many outdoor skills, and camping experience dating back to when she was ten, easily found herself a summer job as a junior camp counselor. Her friend Catherine and several others of their bunch were hired in a group as waitresses at a seaside hotel, where they had fun and good food. A girl who played the piano, and her two friends who were violinists, made up a trio that played supper and dance music at the mountain resort where their families had sometimes been guests and were well acquainted with the management.

One group of girls we know of, in a small city in the

South, canvassed their town to discover what summer jobs needed to be done—then went out and got themselves hired to do the work. They mowed the grass, whitewashed fences and chicken houses, did car washings and a host of other things that imagination and enterprise suggested to them.

The "fresh-air" summer job is certainly the most attractive. If instead you take employment that keeps you indoors in the city, then save yourself at least two weeks before school reopens for a time of rest and real vacation. Don't go back to school next fall tired out, mentally and physically.

If you are a veteran baby-sitter, there are apt to be opportunities for daytime baby-sitting—outdoors in a garden or back yard or park—that appeal to you. One girl accepted the offer of a family who knew and trusted her, to go along with them to their mountain cottage and help relieve the mother of some of the strain of looking after the four small children. She had plenty to do—but she also had a daily dip in the lake and fun with other young people she met during her hours of recreation.

How to make your money count. "Let's stop at the Sugar Bowl for a sundae," Pat suggested, as she and Jean walked home from school.

"Okay, if you'll lend me a quarter," Jean said. "I earned four dollars baby-sitting this week, but I haven't a cent left. Wherever does money go?"

That's a good question. If Jean had had a budget, a system for managing her money, she would have known the answer. Being thrifty doesn't mean putting all your money in the bank and doing without like a miser. It means handling your money so that you are able to buy what you *really* want.

Why not make a plan based on your weekly allowance or

earnings? You will have to work it out for several months at a time in order to allow for future expenses—gifts, for instance, or the Easter trip your class is planning—as well as daily costs. You might provide yourself with a set of small labeled boxes into which you put money for "contributions," "lunches," "entertainment," "snacks," etc.

You won't need to make bookkeeping a permanent part of this operation, but for a couple of weeks, keep careful account of every penny you spend. Only in this way, can you track down everything that consumes your quarters and dimes and find out what expenses are absolutely necessary (fixed expenses) and what are not (flexible expenses).

The important thing in good management of money is to learn the following facts:

1—Your personal way of living and your special desires.
2—Your exact income, not what you wish it were.
3—Your fixed expenses (no fairy with a wand will wave these away).
4—Your personal aims.

After these first two weeks of fact finding, make a tentative plan for the next two weeks. Estimate your income—allowance, earnings, or both. Remember you spend some money daily, some weekly, and some on special occasions, so you will have to divide your income to take care of future expenses as well as daily ones. List your fixed costs—possibly school lunches, dues, church contributions, etc. Then put down your flexible expenses—cosmetics, school supplies, gifts, hobbies, etc. At the end of the two week period, compare your plan with the actual amount of money you have spent. Now you are ready to set up your permanent plan of money management. Keep your special aims in mind. Each of us has a different idea of what constitutes a luxury we can do without. Few of us at any time in our lives have all the money we would like to spend. The satisfaction in handling money well is in making it stretch to cover personal goals.

We have not yet said anything about the law—but you probably know there *are* laws concerning the work of teen-agers. If you are under sixteen, you will need working papers before you can take a part-time or Saturday job while school is in session. State laws cover all employment that is strictly "local"—but vacation permits are usually issued to minors fourteen and over for summer jobs where conditions are approved. Federal law controls work in any industry that transports the goods it manufactures across state lines—this means that until you are eighteen you are not eligible for work in most factories, even when school is closed. The reason, of course, is your own protection against health and safety hazards.

There is the story—but by no means all of it. You must write the rest. What you do to earn money, how you do it, where and when—and the mark it makes on your future life in joyful memories, mature living, vocational discovery —is all for you to work out for yourself.

CHAPTER TEN

YOUR FUTURE

Can I have a career and a happy marriage too?
How can I discover the sort of work that really
    appeals to me? Must I decide soon?
Is there a way to get to college if my parents
    can't meet the expense?
Does a career help a girl to meet the man who can
    make her happy?
When is the right time to marry?

"It isn't easy to decide what you want to be when you're only thirteen," Reba said with a sigh. "Mother insists I ought to go to college and have a career. She admires women who make a success of something; she'll be disappointed if I don't. Dad says he doesn't care."

"And what do you say?"

"I just don't know! I like a lot of things—but nothing too *special*. I suppose I'll get married some day. But Mother says even if you do you should have something to fall back on. I wish I could decide soon, so she wouldn't worry. But I'm just not interested in anything in particular."

Of course you're not, Reba. And there are many, many girls like you. Your high school days should be spent in getting a clear picture of yourself—learning to believe in yourself, developing your interests and hobbies, having girl friends and boy friends. As you grow toward maturity, the rest will take care of itself.

It is a good thing to be thinking about the future—but not to be making firm decisions before you are ready for them. Then, too, some of the confusion and anxiety that girls feel today is due to the fact that women's activities have been so rapidly changing. There was a time, not so very long ago, when girls were not expected to have careers, and a woman who wanted to work after marriage was frowned upon. Much of that has been swept away. But you are just beginning to dream of romance, and you sense that men, especially very young men whose dreams run in the same direction, admire femininity.

Thinking about a career. Without deciding on your future, there are many things you can do right now to help you reach *later* decisions that are right for you. For one thing, you should get into a few extracurricular activities that interest you: like joining the nature club, the camera club, the dramatic club—or being in the high school orchestra or on the school paper. The things you go out for will be an indication of what you like best and might wish to pursue further. Give your hobbies a test run in high school—all and any of them. Some you may drop, because you discover that your interest in them is not so great as you imagined. Others will prove so fascinating that you cling to them through all the four years.

Sometimes a hobby develops into a lifetime activity that makes your whole future bright. If you think of a career as merely a way to make money, it will turn out to be pretty boring, and your "success" will not be worth it. Your *real* success will be in doing things because you dearly love to do them, whether that means keeping house for a family and rearing fine children—a career in itself—or developing an extra line, as so many girls now do, and bringing the mental enrichment it gives you, and the money it earns, to the betterment of family life.

We know a girl whose teen-age hobbies were skin diving and collecting beautiful sea shells on the beaches of southern California where she lived. She was very popular with her gang, because she always seemed to be having fun, and her enthusiasm was catching. Later she went to college and took a liberal arts course. But even then she could not decide what she wanted to be—until it suddenly came to her that sea shells—the little creatures of the ocean—were what she cared about most. And is there any career in that? Of course. The next thing you know, she's a student at the University of Hawaii. "You could call it going to school," she says. "But diving in the Hawaiian surf for sea shells is the greatest fun anyone ever had!" She is now a conchologist—a "sea scientist," with a future that fairly glows with successful achievement *plus* romance.

Stop thinking about your future as something "necessary" and necessarily dull. Be an explorer during the high school years—exploring yourself. Get into all the little inlets and back bays, and find out what you are really like.

A second way to explore your aptitudes is through work out of school. It may be a part-time job or a summer job —and during the teen years you can drop one you don't like and find one you like better, for the more occupations you dip into the better perspective you will have on what the future has to offer in activities that are interesting. Constancy in job holding right now has no great merit. We don't mean to say that you should not be faithful and responsible in any job while you are holding it. But changes are your privilege, for they provide you with your opportunity for looking around.

Edith's mother had been a schoolteacher, and loved it. She took it for granted that Edith would love it, too. She was very much pleased when her daughter took a summer job as a playground aide. But Edith was a quiet girl, who had always loved books and reading. She discovered that summer that work with children was not her bent, though she went through with it conscientiously. During the winter she had a chance to be a library aide. The quiet atmosphere, the daily contact with books and with people who had tastes similar to her own provided a window into the future.

The man for you. There is still a third important path toward self-understanding and self-discovery. And that is through your social life. You will not be spending your future all alone, we hope—but in close relationship with others. Especially, right now, you may be dreaming of the man you may someday marry, and what he will be like. When he comes along, how shall you know that he is "the one?" A great many marriages go on the rocks because a boy and girl are swept away by the glamour of romance, but awaken in a long dreary future to the truth that they have very little in common.

Just as jobs are experimental during the teen years, so are your friendships with boys experimental. Their purpose should be to give you a look into many kinds of personalities. Boys, too, have their hobbies and tastes, and aptitudes for different kinds of occupation. In your social life—dances, parties, clubs—you will have a chance to see what sort of nature accords best with yours. The library aide may adore the high school football hero—at a distance. She may be swept off her feet by the good looks and lively disposition of that hot-rodder who is dating her. But would she be happy for years and years of her future with one of these, unless he shared her viewpoints and goals in life?

Of course the two boys mentioned may have other interests than sports and hot-rods. That's something to find out. One of them, for instance, may develop a strong interest in science through the high school science club. He might even combine interest in science with love of outdoor life—and be just the right sort for the girl who became a "sea scientist."

The point is that only when you know yourself thoroughly, and the boy you admire knows himself thoroughly, can you both be certain what a future together would really be like. The movie or TV romance may end with the "big clinch," just as the old fairy tales ended with "and so they lived happily ever after." But reality begins where fiction leaves off. Don't be misled by a passing "crush"; make sure that your future is filled to overflowing with the happy companionship of someone whose interests you can share, and who shares yours.

Very often a high school girl asks how she can capture the attention of a boy who never looks at her, but with whom she is "in love." All too often such a girl's notion of love is culled from the movies and TV. All the same, there is no real harm in using some discreet means of getting to know the boy, if only to dispel the illusion.

Maidie had a crush like that on Phil, a good-looking and popular youth who sat across the room from her in study hall. Maidie was artistic, loved to draw and paint; sometimes, instead of struggling with her algebra or French lesson, she sketched Phil's finely chiseled features in the back of her notebook. She dreamed about Phil continuously but even if they ran into each other in the hall, he never seemed to see her.

Finally, with the connivance of her best girl friend, Maidie had a few boys and girls at her home one evening, to dance to records—and Phil was included. He came, but acted bored, for he did not dance. That was all right with Maidie, but when she tried to sound him out on his interest in art, he was quite definite. "A lot of tomfoolery," he declared. "All right for bird brains, but not for me." When asked what did interest him, he laughed and said, "Mouse-traps." Seeing her puzzlement, he explained. "You know how they say, 'Build a better mousetrap than anybody else, and people will beat a path to your door.' Well, I figure if I try hard enough I'll find that mousetrap—something that will sell and make me a fortune. Money is what makes the world go round, and I'm going to get my share of it. What do you bet I end up rich?"

He was a nice enough boy, but not for Maidie. She did not care much about ending up rich. It was not her goal. She decided that Phil would be better for some girl who, like him, dreamed of wealth and prestige. When Phil asked her for a date, she managed to make an excuse.

Sometimes high school activities do lay the foundation for a romance that will endure. When Beth went to work on the high school paper, she was overjoyed because she hoped to become a writer. Then she was thrown into constant association with Harold. His chief interest was not writing, but photography. He took many pictures at school and around town that the paper published, and sometimes Beth wrote the little feature stories that accompanied them. Harold was always pleased, telling her that she had caught the mood he had hoped to put into the picture.

The summer she was seventeen, Beth landed a job on the town newspaper as a copy girl. From there she hoped, after college, to rise to work as a regular reporter, and the city editor encouraged her. One day she asked the editor to look at some of Harold's photographs. When her boy friend dropped by for an interview, he was hired, part-time, on the photographic staff.

Those two both went to college, later married, and made a wonderfully happy pair. They had something to build on, and they knew it, for they had tried it out. And the good part was that though each was interested in the other's work, they were not in competition. Competition has killed many a romance, where both were striving for success in the identical field. It need not do so—if both are sufficiently mature not to give way to jealousy. That, too, is something that requires a period of time to explore.

When is the right time to marry? That depends. You don't necessarily need to wait until the young man has acquired a fat bank roll. There are young couples who have struggled through tough times together, and come out on the bright side, loving each other more for all they have been through. But you do need to wait until both are sufficiently mature to face the future realistically. If the young man must forego a college education and the career he had set his heart on, in order to support a wife and family, it is too soon to marry—and the future may yield a harvest of regrets.

And you? Are you ready for the responsibilities of motherhood? It is a question to ask yourself.

During the last war, the infant mortality rate rose sharply across the United States. It was computed by some experts that more babies died than fighting men. When Dr. Leona Baumgartner, of the New York City Board of Health was queried on the cause, she said, "The mothers are too young and inexperienced in baby care."

You see, romance is fine, and getting married is wonderful

—but motherhood is a job. It is too soon to marry unless you are prepared for it. If your high school, or any other group in your town has a course in baby care, do take it. But beyond that, remember that you must have the character, the sense of responsibility, the willingness to forego many pleasures, and to make many sacrifices, in order to be a good mother.

The Girl Scout Michigan Study showed that 96 per cent of all the girls queried hoped to marry. A goal that looms as important as that in the minds of virtually all girls is worth preparation and careful reflection—it is not something for hasty and impulsive action.

Many girls feel that military service forces them either to hasty action or the loss of the young man they love. He is apt to be sent to a camp far away, and letter writing, always a chore, is no substitute for frequent dates. In the new setting, too, he may meet some other girl he likes better and so be lost!

Yes, it's a risk. Much depends on the reality of the bond between you. Many young men have carried their dream of the girl back home through long absences, especially when the two had much in common and a true basis for lifetime happiness. When that exists, there is little to fear. And there is another side to the picture. Many young girls have married hastily and followed their young draftee husbands to some town near the camp, only to find themselves living in almost unimaginable conditions, three and four in a room in a rooming house. Love does not always survive such a test—and if a baby announces itself, the situation can be a tragic one.

Young men who are planning on college frequently feel they would like to get their military service over with first, and then go ahead with their college work when they are more mature. Those with good scholastic standing may prefer to take advantage of arrangements that defer them as long as they keep their college grades high. With the great need for technicians, deferment of those who are headed for training in the technical fields is government policy. All this is something which should be decided in the interests of the young man himself. If you care deeply about him, you will prove it by not pushing him to a decision based wholly on your own desires.

Though the Girl Scout Michigan Study showed marriage as the greatest of all feminine goals, it also revealed that one girl in every three hopes to continue her education after high school—in college, in a secretarial school, in nursing school, in a teachers training college. She may be thinking of a long-range career, or merely of interim employment that will fill the period between high school and marriage and permit her to accumulate a nest egg for later on. Frequently a career interest develops late, as a result of a hobby or a part-time job, but she finds herself blocked in seeking further preparation by the fact that she did not take the high school courses necessary for admission to the institution of her choice.

We are thinking of Sue, who worked in her local hospital as a nurse's aide. She became so interested in nursing as a career that she decided to go on to nursing school. What was her disappointment when she was refused admission because she had not had science. She cared enough to go back and make up the deficiency—but it lost her a year during which other girls she knew were going ahead.

What about college? At thirteen or fourteen you may not have decided on any sort of permanent plans for the future. All the same, it is wise not to slam the door behind you. If there is any likelihood that you *may* wish to con-

tinue your education after high school, get your teacher's
or your student adviser's help in planning a program that
will make college admission possible. The ninth grade is
not too soon to begin thinking about that.

Colette's mother was a graduate of one of the leading
women's colleges of the East. Colette looked forward to
going there, too, and of course being the daughter of an
alumna she felt sure she would have no trouble getting in.
She started off right, from her first year in high school, with
a curriculum that included English, social studies, math,
science, and French.

Toward the end of her sophomore year she began to
worry. She heard that many more girls were trying to get
into her mother's old school than they could take and that
to be admitted you had to be some sort of super-genius.
Her grades were good, but not perhaps at the genius level.
Then there were those college entrance board exams that
had to be passed and from what everybody told her about
them, they were terrible. Would she make it? Just suppose
she failed, and broke her mother's heart and her own as
well?

Besides, there was a third misgiving that added itself to
these two. Her father was a businessman, who recently,
through ill health, had gone into bankruptcy. He had
started all over again, and her mother was working along
with him to help him recuperate the family's fortunes. But
with only two years before she would be ready to go,
Colette wondered if her parents would be able to meet the
high cost of her college education.

She dared not mention her worries at home, but one day
she did lay them bare to her student adviser. Miss Taylor
was a wise woman. She listened patiently, then, with a
smile, she said, "Well, now, you have a whole sheaf of

problems, Colette. Let's take them one at a time and work our way through them."

She called for Colette's school record and looked it over carefully. "It's not bad," she said. "I doubt if you'll be the valedictorian when you graduate—but sometimes the one who is has missed out on activities that are equally important. I'm glad you've been having a well-rounded high school experience. Keep up the good work in your classes and I shall have no doubt about your being ready for college."

"You mean I could pass the college boards all right?"

"Yes—but I'd advise you to take them next year, Colette."

"In my junior year?"

"Almost everyone does. If you pass them then, your worry is over. I think probably you can. But if you don't, you can take them again when you're a senior—and with a better idea of what is expected of you. The second time you are sure to make it."

Colette sighed. "Still—there's the money, Miss Taylor. After I do all that, maybe I can't go anyhow."

Miss Taylor was thoughtful. "Collette," she inquired, "*must* you go to one of the most expensive colleges in the United States, simply because your mother was a student there?"

Colette was astonished. "Why, I just can't imagine going anywhere else," she admitted.

"Why not?"

"Well, you just wouldn't be proud of a diploma from some college no one ever heard about!"

"Is it the diploma you are after—or the education? If it's education, there are hundreds of smaller colleges all over this country that are doing a wonderful educational job. In some of the best small colleges, tuition is quite reasonable. Then there are the state universities, where tuition is free—and they are obliged to admit you, if you reside within the state. You could go to our state university, Colette, and have only your board and incidental expenses to meet."

"It would be an awful comedown, Miss Taylor," Colette confessed.

"Think it over," Miss Taylor advised. "Talk it over with your parents. There is still plenty of time before you need to make a decision."

Colette did think it over. She decided she could not burden her parents with having to send her to a big-name college. When she told them how she felt, she was happy to see their sense of relief. "You're the best little sport in the world, Colette!" her dad exclaimed. And her mother added, "She has character—that's what counts!" For Colette, their praise was her reward.

Maybe you, too, want to go to college—but are worrying about whether your grades will get you in; whether you can pass the college entrance board exams; whether your parents can pay for your college education.

Worry will not get you anywhere. But planning will. Review your high school schedule to make sure you are taking the necessary subjects for admission. Start sending for college catalogues—or study them in your library. Talk with your parents, and those who can advise you at school. In the eleventh grade, take the College Board scholastic aptitude tests and achievement tests and see how you rate in them. Keep up your grades, for they will count as much toward college admission as College Boards—even more so in some schools.

It is true there will be great pressure on the colleges in the next decade, when the number of applicants is expected to double. But it seems certain that those who really wish to go to college will get in—if they do not all insist on going to the big-name schools.

Tuition costs are high—and rising. They vary, from over $2,000 a year in the big-name colleges, to as little as $700 in some of the best smaller ones, while the state universities are tuition-free for state residents, though board and other expenses must be paid.

This may sound frightening to the girl with small resources, but it need not. For there never was a time when scholarships, part-scholarships, and grants-in-aid were so available. Upwards of a million boys and girls are receiving financial help. Here's what you can count on:

College sponsored scholarships are available in nearly 2,000 junior and senior colleges, teachers colleges and universities. For information concerning them, write to College Scholarship Service, Box 176, Princeton, N. J., or Box 27896, Los Angeles 27, California. Scholarship aid is granted in proportion to the family's financial requirements.

National Merit Scholarships are sponsored by a large number of industrial firms. A qualifying test is held each October, and you can register through your own high school principal.

General Motors Scholarships. These include four-year grants up to $2,000 annually to boys and girls entering some 200 colleges participating in the General Motors "College Plan." Ask the college of your choice if it is in this plan. There is also a General Motors "National Plan" by which 100 full four-year scholarships up to $2,000 annually are granted high school seniors on the basis of their scholastic records plus competitive exams.

State scholarships for teacher education are available in thirty states. Find out if yours is one of them.

Scholarships for science education are available in enormous numbers. If this field interests you, write for information to the National Science Foundation, Washington, D. C.

These are just a sampling of the scholarships available. There are thousands more—sponsored by nationality groups, church groups, men's and women's organizations. The United States Congress, concerned with the need for more and more college-trained men and women in our democracy, is making large sums available. Write the U. S. Office of Education, Department of Health, Education and Welfare, Washington, D. C., and ask for information about federal aid for your college education. And make up your mind to this: if you want to go to college today, you can.

Be your own researcher. While you are canvassing the field of colleges and scholarships, read all you can about careers that might interest you. There are thousands of openings for women today, in addition to such things as teaching, secretarial work, and nursing, which you hear about more frequently. There are places for qualified college graduates in teaching, in engineering, in the United States foreign service and civil service, in medicine, in agriculture, in publishing. In many of them, a girl may meet something she did not expect—the added bonus of romance and marriage with a man who is really the "right one."

Incidentally, it could just happen, as you find your place in the thrilling modern world of high endeavor, that the man whose mind and character attract you wears a blue collar rather than a white one. Even as you forsook the idea that only the big-name colleges count, forsake the notion that only the white collar worker has "prestige." There are wonderful men, with brains and inventiveness and high intellect in all the branches of our labor force today—many of them earning high wages because of their skills. One of them may well be the "right man" to fill your life with happiness to overflowing.

Work at something you love. Marry someone you are sure you love. It is the best prescription we know for happiness.

CHAPTER ELEVEN

ROAD MAP

*Can you fill in a portrait of YOU, ten years from
      now? What traits of character does it show?
What is your private prescription for achieving
      happiness?
Have you a road map for reaching the destination
      of your choice?
What do you do about others who get in your way,
      block your path with ambitions of their own?
      Are there "rules of the road"?*

We all want to be successful—not necessarily wealthy or
famous—but successful as persons. And that means to have
a rich, full life, to be loved, respected, admired by those
around us. It sometimes takes a good many years of living
to realize that by themselves beauty, wealth, social position,
fame will not bring us these things we covet. Sometimes
we choose the wrong way to go about gaining them—and
then we blame life or our bad luck when we are unhappy.

Molly was an attractive redhead. Her parents were hard-
working immigrants who barely managed to support the
family. From her earliest teens, Molly made up her mind
to be successful. By her standards this meant earning a
big salary in an important job. When she graduated from
high school, she joined a large corporation. Unceasingly

she worked, planned, schemed to become its most important woman executive. "All's fair in war," she told herself, "and this is my battle." If it meant advancement for her, she did not hesitate to usurp the duties assigned to others, undermine and betray her fellow workers. True, she did not spare herself. No amount of extra hours in the office or office work at home dismayed her, in her willingness to give all her energy to the realization of her ambition.

She married and became a mother, but she had little time to devote to the happiness of her husband and daughter because she still gave all her attention—mind, energy and heart—to the achievement of her goal.

She made it, of course, as such single-minded persons usually do. But she had no real friends—her fellow workers hated and feared her; her husband and child built their own lives without her.

Many people might envy Molly's success, but many others would think it an empty thing, which could not compensate for all she missed in life. Ambition is a good thing, they would say, but not when it becomes an obsession to which all else is sacrificed.

Poets and preachers talk about "the journey of life" and "life's goals." We laugh and say "those old clichés!" But you can't control the direction of your life unless you know where you want to go. It is in this power to direct his life—his will, his ability to reason, to form judgments and to make decisions—that man differs from the animals.

And you—what is your "heart's desire?" Is it to be famous, to be rich, to get into the right social set, to hold an important position in which you can boss others? Is it to have a career, to marry and have children, to serve others? Or a combination of these?

Before you can map out the way for yourself you need

to consider where you are going—find out what you want out of life. This is something you must do for yourself. No one can hand it to you like the map of New England you ask for at a gasoline station.

Now you are beginning to take the command of your life into your own hands. Little by little you have been getting to know yourself. You have been thinking of the kind of person you want to be and trying to live up to this ideal. Being human, you have been disappointed by failures, as we all are from time to time. That's nothing to dismay you, so long as your spirit remains undefeated. You are learning from these mistakes, growing in wider, warmer human sympathy.

The picture of the kind of woman you want to be someday will influence your thoughts and actions now. Likewise the girl you are today and the decisions you make each day—the things you do or do not do—will affect the woman you will be tomorrow. Out of these decisions and actions will emerge your vision of your "life's goals" and the way you should go about achieving them. Your personal values give meaning to your life, and your standards help you to direct it.

Maybe you are willing to leave fame and fortune to the Mollys, if only your life may be a happy one. Our forefathers, writing a constitution for a free people, elevated "the pursuit of happiness" to a central position among the goals of human beings. They saw it as an important end toward which everyone had a right to strive.

But what is happiness? It does not always mean the same thing to you and to others. You are disturbed when you see the sorrows and troubles in the world around you. People who are oppressed, insecure, whose ambitions have failed, whose marriages have broken up, whose fortunes have faded, who are beset by illness. Will any of these things happen to you? Is there any way to insure against such disasters?

The great religions have pointed a way. The Koran says: "Happiness must be earned." The Bible tells us, "Give and it shall be given unto you." What they are saying is that if you think more of others than of yourself you will have a happier life. No one can be insulated from the trials and misfortunes that may occur in a lifetime. It is the way a person meets them, his philosophy of life, that makes the difference.

Now is the time for you to begin to develop those resources that will help you bear successfully whatever may come of good or evil.

One girl in her teens said, "I want to use my life to make as many people as possible happy. I want to find and develop my talents and not waste them. I want to have a good relationship with other people who respect me as I do them, regardless of race, religion, or social status." She was thinking of giving rather than getting.

This ideal of *giving*—of service to others—does not mean forsaking your dream of meeting and marrying a man who loves you sincerely and can make you happy; nor your ambition to become a writer or painter, musician or actress, nurse or fashion designer. There is no room in a happy life for self-imposed martyrdom. Instead, think of yourself as a unique personality, different from everyone else in the world, with "gifts" you are meant to cultivate for the sake of others.

Most marriages, along with love and romance, offer an opportunity for a lifetime of service and self-forgetfulness. Service to husband, to children, sometimes to old and feeble parents, to friends and neighbors in need. It is the wife who gives freely of her love for the benefit of those about her who is apt to find happiness, rather than the one who constantly demands fresh proof that she is loved.

The same thing is true in a career. A great actress like Helen Hayes has given years of hard study and ceaseless effort to the task of bringing joy to others; she is happier to have succeeded in that than to see her name in electric lights.

Examine your values. Seek to be true to your inner self. Decide what is your idea of successful living, and follow that road with as few detours as you can manage.

You need faith in God, in life, in yourself. You need to find your reason for living, or something to live by, a guide to the way.

Each of us must find the way for herself. Three generations of girls have found it in the Girl Scout Promise and Laws, which have been to them a satisfying way of life and a sound and helpful code of ethics.

> On my honor, I will try:
> To do my duty toward God and my country,
> To help other people at all times,
> To obey the Girl Scout laws.

To do my duty toward God. Do you do honor to God in the things you think, say and do in the faithful practice of your religion? The major religions all teach that we show love and gratitude to God in the way we behave toward each other. Do you acknowledge that all men, of whatever nationality, creed or race, are your brothers, and try to treat them as you would wish to be treated?

And to my country. Does your duty to your country mean more to you than just honoring the flag? Does it mean respecting its traditions and obeying its laws? Do you seek to learn about the past of your country and other countries, and about what is taking place in the world at present, so that you will be an informed citizen and voter? Do you give thought to what you can do to make your country a better place in which to live—a place in which all people may live and work in safety and freedom?

And help other people at all times. Do you think of others rather than yourself? Do you learn skills you can share with others? Do you try to observe in small ways courtesy, generosity, and friendliness? Do you look for opportunities to help others in big and little ways?

If you are a Girl Scout, think about your Promise and the Laws you promised to keep as a guide for daily living. If you are not a Girl Scout, give the Girl Scout Promise serious consideration. Use it as a guide in forming your own personal code.

While you are drafting your own guide to successful living, ask yourself how you feel about honor, loyalty, usefulness, obedience—old-fashioned abstractions that still rate high in the space age. Do you tell the truth, play fair? Do your work honestly, safeguard other people's money, possessions, confidences? Do you keep your promises? Is your honor to be trusted?

What about loyalty? Do you stand up for the things you think are right and good? Are you faithful to your family, your friends, your school, your country, your religion?

Most of us like to be needed, to be useful. Do you take on your share of duties at home, in school, or wherever you may be?

How do you feel toward your fellow men? Are you filled with good will toward all people, regardless of nationality, creed, or color—and are you active in demonstrating this?

We like to be with people who are courteous and cheerful. Are you thoughtful of other people's feelings? Are you considerate of others, although their ways of living and their beliefs may differ from your own? Are you pleasant and happy as you go about your daily jobs? Do you try not to become discouraged when things seem hard? Try not to grumble when things don't go your way?

We respect the person who obeys orders. Do you obey the laws of your community, the rules of your school, and the requests of people who are in authority over you?

What about thrift? Do you use your time and your money wisely, so that you have them when you need them and can spare some for others? Are you careful of your own and other people's things—your notebooks, your school desk, possibly your employer's paper, pencils, telephone calls?

Do you direct your thoughts to worthwhile things, so that you do not stoop to words or deeds that would make you ashamed of yourself or make others ashamed of you?

As you go about your daily living, you are adding to your personal road map. Whether it runs straight and true or is fouled up in detours and bypasses depends on the skill, you, the cartographer, bring to its designing. The ideals, the values, the standards that you are choosing to follow today will have much to do with molding the future You, and with the kind of ethical heritage you will pass on to your children.

Don't be solemn about it. Away with "past regrets and future fears." Enjoy the present moment to the utmost. Life was meant to be met with zest and joy. May your journey be happy and the detours few.

ASK YOURSELF THESE QUESTIONS

Correct answers to each main group give you a rating of 20—to all five groups a rating of 100.

I. *ABOUT YOURSELF* (Counts 20)

Score
1 for each
correct
answer

You as a Person (6 points)

1. Your personality ☐ never changes; ☐ changes during adolescence; ☐ changes throughout life....
2. If people treat you like a baby you should: ☐ assert your independence; ☐ refuse to do chores; ☐ stop acting babyish ....
3. Puberty means ☐ youth; ☐ adolescence; ☐ sexual maturity ....
4. Menarche means ☐ motherly instincts; ☐ interest in men and boys; ☐ beginning of menstruation ....
5. During menstruation it is ☐ dangerous to bathe; ☐ safe to go swimming; ☐ safe to take a daily warm bath ....
6. You can develop your breasts ☐ by proper exercise; ☐ by eating fattening foods; ☐ not at all....

142

Your Looks   (7 points)

1. *Complexion* is improved by ☐ removal of pimples and blackheads; ☐ use of good cosmetics; ☐ regular bathing, diet, sleep, exercise..........

2. *Hair styles:* (Fill in blanks with face shapes—round, long, or pointed.)
   A pompadour with flat side hair suits a
   ....face;
   Curls at nape of neck are good with a
   ....face;
   Bang and fluffy side curls suit a
   ....face............................

3. *Dress Styles:* (Fill in blanks with fat, thin, flat-chested)
   Darker tones and slightly flared skirts are for the .... girl;
   Bright tones, contrasting blouse with a full skirt suit the .... girl;
   Fluffy blouses, big collars, dickies are becoming to a .... girl ....

4. *A Fat Girl* should ☐ go on a 10-day diet of lettuce and tomatoes; ☐ eat balanced meals; ☐ eat less meat and butter ....

5. *Lip Rouge* should ☐ not be worn before age 14; ☐ never be worn to school; ☐ be worn for school or dates according to custom in the community ....

6. *Fingernails* look best when ☐ manicured pointed with red polish; ☐ rounded with pink polish; ☐ matched with toenails in summer ......

7. *Gym Exercises* are important because they improve your ....· ....

Your Manners   (7 points) (No. 1 counts 1 point)

1. For social ease you need *most:* ☐ knowledge of the rules of etiquette; ☐ a home where you can entertain; ☐ a spirit of friendliness . . . .

2. To give a successful party you should: (Note: Choose three of the following that are correct; the remainder are false. For a fully correct answer you *score 3;* otherwise 0.) . . . .

   Plan carefully;

   Follow a prepared schedule of games, dances, refreshments;

   Mail written invitations, requesting replies;

   Be careful not to omit any of your friends;

   Keep refreshments and decorations simple;

   Ignore a guest who starts a bit of roughhouse;

   Let lovebirds retreat to a corner if they wish;

   Be sure to introduce a late guest to all present;

   Put a shy guest to work helping you.

3. Good table manners require you to: (Note: Choose three of the following that are correct— the rest are false; you score either 3 or 0.) . . . .

   Swallow an oyster in an oyster cocktail whole;

   Break your bread in small pieces and butter it as you eat it;

   Take some of everything served you;

   Break the crackers served you into your soup;

   When served a large sandwich, eat it without cutting;

   Apologize profusely if you spill something.

II. *YOUR FRIENDS*   (Counts 20)

Girl Friends   (5 points)   Score 1 for
                                        each correct answer

1. You will be popular if you always take the lead
   in good times and activities   ☐ True; ☐ False....
2. You should try to go along with the bunch in
   the fun they plan   ☐ True; ☐ False....
3. You should refuse to do anything that is contrary to your personal standards

                                  ☐ True; ☐ False....
4. You do better to stick to one best girl friend,
   rather than a whole group   ☐ True; ☐ False....
5. You can make many friends by sharing your
   skills   ☐ True; ☐ False....

Boy Friends   (15 points)

1. You will make more boy friends if you get into
   high school hobby clubs   ☐ True; ☐ False....
2. A boy likes only sophisticated girls

                                  ☐ True; ☐ False....
3. A blind date is all right if the boy is known to
   your family or friends   ☐ True; ☐ False....
4. A boy who takes you out should not expect a
   kiss   ☐ True; ☐ False....
5. A good-night kiss at your door or on special
   occasions is harmless   ☐ True; ☐ False....
6. Necking and petting are necessary if a girl
   wishes to be popular   ☐ True; ☐ False....
7. Petting is a dangerous practice that can lead
   to serious trouble   ☐ True; ☐ False....
8. If a boy you don't like asks you for a date, stall

him in the hope that someone better will turn
up   ☐ True; ☐ False....

9. Going steady is unwise, as it limits your acquaintance with boys   ☐ True; ☐ False....

10. For some girls, going steady is the best plan
     ☐ True; ☐ False....

11. If a boy hands you a line, you should ☐
squelch him hard; ☐ hand him back a line ......

12. If a group of high school boys give you the
wolf whistle, you should ☐ stare coldly to
show you are insulted; ☐ smile in friendly
fashion as you walk past; ☐ toss them a wisecrack to show you have a sense of humor ....

13. Going Dutch is a fine idea   ☐ True; ☐ False....

14. Curfew for dates while in high school should
be not later than 11 p.m.   ☐ True; ☐ False....

15. Early marriage is advisable if the boy you love
is leaving for a distant camp
     ☐ True; ☐ False....

III. *HOME AND FAMILY* (Counts 20)

> Note: Each group gives you *4 points*
> if answered correctly; score *1
> point* for each correct part.

Your Parents (4 points) ....Score....

Only three of the following five statements are
true. Pick the true ones:

1. Your parents do not always know what is best
for you.

2. They have a right to query you on all your
activities.

3. They should expect you to take responsibility for home chores.
4. They should go out for the evening if you give a party.
5. They should expect you to baby-sit younger children occasionally.

Your Clothes (4 points) ....Score....

Only three of the following five statements are true. Pick the true ones:

1. You have a right to select all your own clothes.
2. Your mother should decide what clothes are best for you.
3. You should ask mother's advice, but make the choice yourself.
4. Slacks are better than frills for some occasions.
5. A party dress is easy to make at home.

Your Dates (4 points) ....Score....

Only three of the following five statements are true. Pick the true ones:

1. You should be permitted dates with boys for school parties in junior high.
2. Your parents do not always have to know where you are going on a date.
3. You should not date boys until you are fourteen.
4. You should observe the curfew hour your parents set.

5. You should telephone home if you change your plans or are delayed.

Your Allowance   (4 points) ....Score....

Only three of the following five statements are true. Pick the true ones:

1. Your allowance should be sufficient for all your needs—school, church, clothes, recreation.
2. Your allowance should meet daily expenses; your parents paying for big items like clothes.
3. You'll be happier if you earn part of what you spend.
4. Money you earn you are free to spend as you please.
5. It's wise to budget and plan ahead for extras you may desire.

Your Brothers and Sisters   (4 points) ......Score...

Only three of the following five statements are true. Pick the true ones:

1. A sister should not be allowed to borrow your clothes.
2. You should insist that a younger brother or sister who annoys your guests be punished.
3. An older brother or sister should sometimes be asked for advice and leadership.
4. The best way to settle disputes with younger or older siblings is to talk them over quietly.
5. You should ask your parents for a family conference if troubles with siblings can't be settled.

IV. *YOUR EDUCATION, JOBS, FUTURE CAREER*

(Counts 20)

High School Days (5 points)

Rate yourself 1 on
each correct answer.

1. Earning a diploma is the big thing—skip all the social life and dates ☐ True; ☐ False....
2. Your parents should help you arrange a quiet time for home study ☐ True; ☐ False....
3. Electives are less important; you can choose the ones you find easiest ☐ True; ☐ False....
4. It's wise to plan your program from 9th grade so you can gain admission to college if you decide to go ☐ True; ☐ False....
5. You should plan to do your easiest homework in high school study hall ☐ True; ☐ False....

After-school Jobs (5 points)

1. The money you make is the only advantage of a part-time job ☐ True; ☐ False....
2. A Saturday job is better than one on school days ☐ True; ☐ False....
3. If you accept a job you should stick to it, even if you dislike it ☐ True; ☐ False....
4. A full-time summer job is often preferable to a part-time winter job ☐ True; ☐ False....
5. It's all right for a baby-sitter to have her boy friend in to help her with her math homework ☐ True; ☐ False....

High School Social Life (5 points)

1. Extracurricular activities are an important part of your education ☐ True; ☐ False....

2. You should try to do your homework quickly so as to have time for your social life
□ True; □ False....

3. High school hobbies often point the way to a future career □ True; □ False....

4. High school friendships teach you to get on with other people of both sexes
□ True; □ False....

5. Most high school romances lead to happy marriages □ True; □ False....

College—and a Career (5 points)

1. You don't need college if you expect to marry and make a home □ True; □ False....

2. You should not plan on college if your parents can't meet the expense □ True; □ False....

3. You do not need to decide on a career while in high school □ True; □ False....

4. You can have a happy marriage and a career
□ True; □ False....

5. The career girl is unpopular with boys
□ True; □ False....

V. *LOOKING AHEAD AT YOU* (Counts 20)

Rate yourself 1 on each correct answer.

Your Ideal of Self (5 points)

1. The person you hope to become is the one you probably will be □ True; □ False....

2. Ambition and hard work are the surest roads to success in life □ True; □ False....

3. Happiness is something you can only achieve by effort □ True; □ False....

4. You will be happy if you marry a man who
   loves you   ☐ True; ☐ False....
5. You will be happy if you have a beautiful home
   and fine social position   ☐ True; ☐ False....

Your Standards   (5 points)

1. Famous people are usually very selfish
                                ☐ True; ☐ False....
2. People of every race, color and creed are your
   brothers and sisters   ☐ True; ☐ False....
3. Success lies in what you think of yourself rather
   than in public acclaim   ☐ True; ☐ False....
4. A mature person is eager to give more than he
   gets   ☐ True; ☐ False....
5. Mistakes and failures are nothing to be
   ashamed of   ☐ True; ☐ False....

Your Faith   (5 points)

1. Weekly church attendance is sufficient evidence
   of your faith in God   ☐ True; ☐ False....
2. Service to others is the way to prove your
   gratitude to God   ☐ True; ☐ False....
3. If you sacrifice your precious life goals, God
   will reward you   ☐ True; ☐ False....
4. The only way to treat people who behave badly
   toward others is to ostracize them
                                ☐ True; ☐ False....
5. Your shortcomings will only be mended if you
   treat them with stern severity
                                ☐ True; ☐ False....

The Inner Law—Your Code   (5 points)

1. You should adopt the code of ethics of someone
   you most admire   ☐ True; ☐ False....

2. You cannot follow any code that is not your own   ☐ True; ☐ False. . . .

3. Everyone's ethical code is partly a heritage
                                 ☐ True; ☐ False. . . .

4. The codes of conduct of most great religions show similarity   ☐ True; ☐ False. . . .

5. Your ethical code will mold your life and that of your children   ☐ True; ☐ False. . . .

THE ANSWERS

I. *ABOUT YOURSELF:*

You as a Person: 1. Personality changes throughout life. 2. Stop acting babyish. 3. Puberty means sexual maturity. 4. Menarche is beginning of menstruation. 5. It's safe to take a daily warm bath. 6. Nothing will make your breasts grow until they develop naturally.

Your Looks: 1. *Complexion* is aided by regular bathing, exercise, balanced diet, sleep, exercise. 2. *Hair styles* are: Pompadour for round face; curls at nape of neck for pointed face; bangs for long face. 3. *Dress styles:* Darker tones, flared skirt for fat girl; Bright, contrasting tones for thin girl; Fluffy blouses for flat-bosomed. 4. *A fat girl* should eat balanced meals. 5. *Lip Rouge* should be worn for school and dates at the age and according to the custom in the community. 6. *Fingernails* should be rounded with pink polish; toenails can take a much darker tone. 7. Gym exercises are important because they improve posture.

Your Manners: 1. Spirit of friendliness. 2. Plan carefully; keep refreshments and decorations simple; put a shy guest to work helping you. 3. Good table manners require you to swallow the oyster whole; break your bread in small pieces; take some of everything offered you.

II. *YOUR FRIENDS:*

Girl Friends: 1. False, you should both lead and follow. 2. True, unless it is contrary to your standards. 3. True. 4. False —you may have a close girl friend but should have other friends too. 5. True.

Boy Friends: 1. True, you'll meet boys with similar tastes. 2. False, boys like girls who are natural and fun to be with. 3. True. 4. True—you don't want to kiss every boy. 5. True, a good-night kiss is harmless if you like the boy. 6. False—necking and petting may destroy your popularity. 7. True, petting is most dangerous. 8. False—you must consider the boy's feelings and give him an immediate answer. 9. True, for the teens are the time to get to know more than one boy. 10. True, for the girl who finds it very hard to make boy friends it may prove the best plan for a time. 11. Hand him back a line. 12. Meet the wolf whistle of boys you know with a friendly smile, no wisecracks. 13. False—going Dutch hurts a boy's pride. You reciprocate in other ways. 14. False—curfew hour depends on the occasion and the general practice agreed on in the community. 15. False—if the boy really loves you he won't forget you; better to wait.

III. *HOME AND FAMLY:*

Your Parents: 1. True, your parents do not always know what is best for you. 3. They should expect you to do home chores. 5. They should expect you to baby-sit if they go out occasionally. No. 2 and 4 are false.

Your Clothes: 3, 4 and 5 are correct.

Your Dates: 1, 4, and 5 are correct.

Your Allowance: 2, 3, and 5 are correct. Many families could not provide an allowance large enough to cover everything, but can help with clothes or recreation from time to time. Earned money should be budgeted and spent as carefully as unearned allowance; you need this sort of training.

Your Brothers and Sisters: 3, 4, and 5 are correct. A little borrowing with permission between sisters is usual and friendly. A request for advice is a great softener. Punishment won't help as much as calm talk and leadership, or failing that, a friendly family conference.

IV. *YOUR EDUCATION, JOBS, FUTURE CAREER*

High School Days: 1 and 3 are false. High school is preparation for life, not just for a diploma. Electives should be chosen carefully, to give you cultural background that will enrich your life. 2, 4, and 5 are correct.

After-school Jobs: 1. False—part-time work gives you an opportunity to learn about different jobs and to try out your new adult sense of responsibility. 2. False—the choice depends on the girl; she may like outdoor sports on Saturday; or may prefer to have weekdays free. 3. False—now is your time to explore others you may like better. 4. True—a summer job, particularly if it is outdoors, leaves winter free for study and extracurricular activities. 5. False—baby-sitting is a serious job, not the time for entertaining the boy friend.

High School Social Life: 1, 2, 3, and 4 are correct. 5 is false. Most high school boys and girls do not know themselves well enough to know whether they would be good mates for a lifetime. And often, as they grow older, their personalities change.

College and a Career: 3 and 4 are true; 1, 2, and 5 are false. A college woman may have more in common with her husband, and more to give her children. There are thousands of scholarships available for girls whose parents can't afford college. The career girl often finds a congenial husband through her career.

V. LOOKING AHEAD AT YOU

Your Ideal of Self: 1 and 3 are true. For 2, it depends on your estimate of success—financial success and power are not the true success of the individual, count this one *false*. 4 should also be counted false—it is good to have a loving husband, but you will only be happy if *you* love *him* and can adjust to married life. 5 is false—wealth and social position are not enough to make happiness.

Your Standards: 1 is false. Many people who win fame deserve it because of their unselfish devotion to service through the arts, through human welfare projects, and in other ways. They are not seeking public acclaim—and so 3 is true. True, also, are 2, 4, and 5. Often our mistakes and failures are the means by which we learn.

Your Faith: 1. False. You show your faith in your daily attitude toward God and your fellow man. 2 is true—service to others shows your gratitude to God. 3 is false—God wants you to pursue your life goals, provided they are worthy ones. 4. False. Be true to your own feelings but try to understand and help such people. 5. False. Forgive and forget your shortcomings, and go on to better things; focus on the good. That is the way of faith in yourself.

The Inner Law—Your Code: 2, 3, 4, and 5 are true—but 1 is false. You cannot follow another person's "inner law" unless and until you have made it your own. The same is true of the code you inherit through your family or religion—it only becomes useful as it is accepted by you as worthy of your obedience.